George E. Vandeman

IT IS WRITTEN CLASSICS

LIFE
AFTER
DEATH

GEORGE E. VANDEMAN

Pacific Press Publishing Association
Boise, Idaho
Montemorelos, Nuevo Leon, Mexico
Oshawa, Ontario, Canada

Edited by Ken McFarland
Cover design by Tim Larson
Portrait of George Vandeman by Ilyong Cha
Type set in 10/12 Century Schoolbook

ISBN 0-8163-0646-X

86 87 88 89 90 ● 5 4 3 2

Contents

Section IV: Miscellaneous Messages to Remember

Before You Turn the Page

Reserved for this final volume of "It Is Written" classics are Pastor Vandeman's unique telecast messages that answer your insistent questions about life after death.

Who doesn't want to learn what lies beyond the grave? And why are we bombarded at every supermarket checkout counter with the sensational claims and proposed "answers" of the psychics? Is there a satisfying way to know the truth about the future? Are there answers which provide hope in place of despair? The first three sections that follow will give a resounding *yes* to these questions.

Finally, seven specials on widely different subjects complete this four-volume set of memorable "It Is Written" telecasts. They provide a fitting climax to the wide sweep of Scripture truth revealed in this ministry. *Life After Death!* We promise you it will be rewarding to learn that goodbyes don't have to be final.

Can You
Catch a Soul?

If you wanted to be immortal, would you write a book, establish an orphanage, say a prayer, visit a séance, or consult your family physician?

Or is immortality just a dream that disappears under the strong light of reason—something that could never happen?

Some members of the medical profession are telling us that immortality for the human race may soon be achieved—possibly before the end of the century.

Exciting, isn't it?

The word "immortal," just to refresh your memory, means "not subject to death." In other words, it would be impossible for a person who is immortal to die. Whether such a state would be a blessing or a curse would depend, of course, on the quality of life we are talking about. Immortality, with death an impossibility, would hardly be a blessing to a patient with incurable cancer.

Also, before you get too carried away by the prospect of immortality in the near future, you should know that the immortality medical science hopes soon to achieve is evidently not the kind described in the dictionary. For we are told that possessing this immortality would "not mean that one could abuse the body with unhealthy living habits." We are reminded that "just as a new car can be destroyed in a wreck, so can the delicate chemical machinery of the human body be destroyed, immortality or no immortality. . . . The man of thirty-five who drops dead of a heart attack because of unwise living habits cannot be saved by learning the secrets of immortality. Nor can these secrets protect a person from pneumonia, tuberculosis, and lethal levels of toxic pollutants."

Strange kind of immortality, isn't it? Apparently medical science is talking about nothing more than lengthening our normal life-span.

But even with these limitations, these watered-down possibilities, it is suggested by one medical writer that such an achievement would be a major threat to religion. He says "religions which offered a reward of life everlasting to the faithful would have to face the fact that life everlasting was possible here on earth"—without any assistance or intervention on God's part. It is even suggested that the Soviet Union might be the first to achieve immortality because of its de-emphasis on religious concepts.

What do you think of that?

My Bible tells me that "the wages of sin is death; but the gift of God is eternal life through Jesus Christ our Lord." Romans 6:23, KJV.

And my Bible tells me, "For God so loved the world, that he gave his only begotten Son, that whosoever believeth in him should not perish, but have everlasting life." John 3:16, KJV.

But now comes the suggestion that we don't need the gift of immortality, that the Son of God didn't need to bother dying for us so we could have it—that, thank you, we can manage it very nicely ourselves!

What label do you put on that sort of suggestion? I don't like to call it blasphemy. Maybe it would be kinder just to call it human cockiness. In any case, God has a way of putting us in our place when we go too far!

Is immortality possible? Or is it just a dream born of our natural desire to live?

So we come back to the question, "Aren't we created with an immortal soul—a soul that cannot die?"

"We shall try our best to do as you say," said Crito. "But how shall we bury you?"

And Socrates replied, "Any way you like. That is, if you can catch me and I don't slip through your fingers."

Is there, as Socrates believed, something that slips away when a man dies—something difficult to catch? Is that why some people don't take death seriously?

We don't want to die. We shrink from the horror of not living. It is only natural to try to wish it away, to grasp at any suggestion that death might not be real, that it might be only an unhappy myth.

So it is not surprising that we try to deny it, to explain it away, to find some alternate. The thought of dying, of not existing, has seemed too terrifying to accept without a fight, without setting the mind to invent some theory of the afterlife that is less unpleasant.

The Greek philosophers believed that the soul and the body are entirely separate, that the soul is temporarily imprisoned in the body but is freed from it at death, destined to live on forever. Their concept has been described as that of an angel in a slot machine—the soul good like an angel, the body bad like a slot machine.

Believing as they did, they considered the body very unimportant. It was soon to be shed anyway. The soul, to them, was the real person and would survive death quite all right. Consequently they didn't take death very seriously.

This Greek philosophy has for many centuries influenced the mainstream of Christian thinking. But does the soul leave the body at death and live on? Is the soul destined to live forever—somewhere? Is immortality something that everybody has? Is living forever automatic for everyone, good and bad?

That's what millions believe. And to many the thought that life is destined to continue after death has brought comfort. But surprising as it may seem to some of you, it has brought millions unbelievable oppression!

Long before Jesus was born, Hinduism held India under the iron law of karma. For the Hindu, belief in natural immortality was a cruel and oppressive power. For the Hindu there was no escape from the relentless wheel of karma. He went through his unhappy life believing that he must suffer a life of pain and degradation, only to die and be born again, over and over, suffering the same pain in life after life—with never any hope for relief.

This may be difficult for an American, for instance, to understand. Because many Americans have a way of taking up with a belief almost as a fad—enjoying it while it is popular, and discarding it when they tire of it. Reincarnation and karma have had a season of popularity recently in America. But when the idea loses its novelty, it is easily tossed aside. Not so with the peoples of the East who really believe it, who never think of questioning it. Countless millions would give anything to be free of the terrible burden!

When Buddha came along, he offered his followers escape from mortality. He taught that if a man could achieve the state he called *nirvana*, an experience of perfect serenity, he could wear down the forces of karma and escape the intolerable cycle of being born again and again. So although Buddha brought with him little truth, he did bring some comfort to the lower-caste Hindu of his day.

The early Christian church, in common with some sects of Judaism, believed that when a man died, he died. There was nothing more, except by a specific act on God's part. The early church centered its message around the resurrection of Christ. And the resurrection of Christ was a demonstration of His power to resurrect His people at the last day.

But not long after the death of the apostles, the Christian church was influenced by the teaching of Plato, who said that man never really died, that he couldn't because he had an immortal soul. This was the teaching of Plato, you understand—not that of the Bible.

And then another man-made idea was added. If a man had an immortal soul and couldn't die, and if he wasn't worthy of heaven, he would have to go on living somewhere. So an eternally burning hell was invented.

Here was a new kind of karma. If anything, it was worse. Karma taught endless pain, in life after life. But with an ever-burning hell it was not simply a life of recurring pain; it was endless torture. Countless mothers have wept their hearts out over the thought of a son or a daughter writhing in perpetual torment. And nobody knows how many thousands have turned away from religion entirely because they didn't want to worship so cruel a God.

In spite of this, most of us want to keep on living—forever. And now, as we pointed out earlier, scientists and physicians are investigating the possibility of a man-made immortality that they see as a potential challenge to the promised gift of God.

And then, ever with us, are the psychic groups, the spiritist groups, who are dedicated to proving that man does not die when he dies, and that therefore communication with our lost loved ones is possible.

Confusing, isn't it?

So what is the truth? Did God create man with an immortal soul? Or didn't He?

Could there be a better place to turn than to the inspired record of creation? We read there, "And the Lord God formed man of the dust of the ground, and breathed into his nostrils the breath of life; and man became a living soul." Genesis 2:7, KJV.

Here we are told *how* man was created. God formed a body out of the dust. Then He breathed life into that body. And man *became* a living soul.

Notice that it doesn't say that God *gave* man a living soul. It says that man *became* a living soul. The soul, then, is the whole man, the whole person. It is not some part of man that can float around independent of the body.

The soul is the combination of the body and the breath of life. So what happens when a man dies and the process is reversed? We read, "Then shall the dust return to the earth as it was: and the spirit shall return unto God who gave it." Ecclesiastes 12:7, KJV.

The dust, the body, returns to the earth. It is dust again. And the spirit, or the breath, the breath of life, returns to God. The Hebrew word translated "spirit" also means "breath."

Remember that man became a living soul as the result of the combining of the body and the breath of life. When the combination is broken, when the breath is removed, he is no longer a living soul. He will not be a living soul again until the Creator, at the resurrection, again breathes life into the body, until the combination of body and breath is restored.

Where does the soul go at death? It doesn't go anywhere. It simply ceases to exist *as a soul* until the resurrection day.

Let's illustrate it this way. Suppose that you have an electric light bulb. And you have electric current. When these are combined, you have light. If either is missing—if you have no bulb, or you have no current—you have no light. Where does the light go? It doesn't go anywhere. It just ceases to exist until the combination is restored. Do you see?

Let's look at this question from another angle. Whatever the soul is, it is capable of dying. Because God says through the prophet Ezekiel, "The soul that sinneth, it shall die." Ezekiel 18:20, KJV.

The soul, then, can die. Remember that the soul is the whole man, the whole person. One of the modern translations of this scripture says, "The *person* who sins will die." Ezekiel 18:20, NASB.

Now I am aware that we sometimes use the word "soul" in a different way, as if it were something other than simply the whole person. We say, "I feel it in my soul." We talk about saving a man's soul. And Jesus asked the question, "For what shall it profit a man, if he shall gain the whole world, and lose his own soul? Or what shall a man give in exchange for his soul?" Mark 8:36, 37, KJV.

I am aware, too, that He said, "And fear not them which kill the body, but are not able to kill the soul: but rather fear him which is able to destroy both soul and body in hell." Matthew 10:28, KJV.

But again, here's the point. *Whatever* the soul is, it can die. It can be destroyed. For didn't we just read that *both* soul and body could be destroyed in hell?

We need not be concerned with fine theological distinctions here. We have our answer. Whatever the soul is, it is not immortal. It can die. It can be destroyed.

Back to the book of Genesis again, the account of creation. Shortly after God created Adam, He told him, "Of every tree of the garden thou mayest freely eat: but of the tree of the knowledge of good and evil, thou shalt not eat of it: for in the day that thou eatest thereof *thou shalt surely die*." Genesis 2:16, 17, KJV.

"Thou shalt surely die." Would God say that if He had just hours ago created Adam immortal, incapable of dying? Would He threaten a punishment that He could not possibly carry out?

Evidently the apostle Paul knew nothing about man being incapable of dying, because he said—remember, "For the wages of sin is death." Romans 6:23, KJV.

And remember again that well-loved scripture— John 3:16. God gave His only begotten Son. Why? So that we "should not perish."

Tell me. Why would God need to let His Son die so we wouldn't have to perish—if we were made imperishable, so that we couldn't possibly perish? Ever think of that? If everybody, good and bad, is automatically going to live forever anyway, then nobody needs a Saviour. And if nobody needs a Saviour, then the cross of Calvary was only a meaningless drama!

And the resurrection. The New Testament fairly rings with excitement over the resurrection. Jesus, by walking out of the tomb, had demonstrated that resurrection is possible. He had demonstrated that they, too, could be resurrected—body and all. But why, I ask—why would a resurrection of the body even be needed if the soul could live on happily, independent of it?

Here is perhaps the clearest scripture of all. Paul, speaking of God, says, "Who only hath immortality." 1 Timothy 6:16, KJV.

So God alone has immortality. Evidently even the angels were not created immortal. If they were, then the angels who rebelled along with Satan and were cast out of heaven could never be destroyed.

God is too wise to create His subjects with the power of choice and at the same time make them immortal, incapable of dying. If God had created Adam and Eve immortal, then when they sinned He would have had a race of immortal sinners on His hands. God did not create for Himself any such dilemma. He does not bestow immortality upon any man until he has been tested, until he has proved that he can be trusted with it!

Evidently we are not immortal. We do not have an immortal soul. We can die, and do die. And except for the intervention of Jesus Christ on our behalf, death would be permanent, with no hope of never-ending life.

But Jesus died to change all this. He died to make immortality possible. The apostle Paul says, "Christ Jesus . . . has destroyed death and has brought life and immortality to light through the gospel." 2 Timothy 1:10, NIV.

Our Lord wants us to live forever. His death in our place has made it possible. But we do not receive the gift of immortality *until* He returns. Paul describes it. He says, "Listen, I tell you a mystery: We shall not all sleep, but we shall all be changed—in a flash, in the twinkling of an eye, at the last trumpet. For the trumpet will sound, the dead will be raised imperishable, and we shall be changed. For the perishable must clothe itself with the imperishable, and the mortal with immortality. When the perishable has been clothed with the imperishable, and the mortal with immortality, then the saying that is written will come true: 'Death has been swallowed up in victory.' " 1 Corinthians 15:51-54, NIV.

What a day! That's when our Lord will give the gift of immortality, of never-ending life, to those who have proved they can be trusted with it!

And thank God it will not be like the man-made immortality that some in medical science are envisioning—a so-called immortality that would still be subject to death at the hands of an accident, or a virus, or some other threat. It will be a life that death can never touch. For death itself will have been finally destroyed at the hands of the One who conquered it on Calvary!

Is immortality that medical science hopes to achieve in any sense a threat to Christianity? Hardly!

Life, to be worth living, must have more than one dimension. It must have more than length. There must be a *quality* of life that makes it desirable, attractive, worth having. Changing a man's body without changing his heart is hardly the answer. Nor is changing a man's body without changing his environment anything to get excited about.

Is long life, filled with fear and depression, a thing to be desired? Is prolonging our boredom what we are looking for?

Does lengthening our life-span really mean happiness and peace of mind and security—if death is still around? If we are still subject to death by virus or by violence, is that immortality? Would lengthening the life-span of criminals, so that they could be repeatedly paroled to the streets—would that solve the crime problem? If men, with their present life-span, have split the atom and stockpiled weapons that fill us with indescribable horror, what would happen if men lived a thousand years?

Living longer and longer—in a world growing worse and worse. Is that a life to be desired? No, friend. In such a situation suicide would be common. Death, to many, would seem not an enemy but a friend.

Life, you see, *can be* an intolerable burden. Millions of Tibetans could tell you that!

Beyond This Day

Long, silent hours. Guards keep their quiet, careful vigil beside the Tomb of the Unknown Soldier.

If the Unknown Soldier could speak, what would he tell of the unknown? Is he aware of the changing of the guard? Is he conscious of the honor heaped about his memory through the silent, respectful years?

Is there some sort of psychic telephone by which we can talk with this honored victim of war? And if some enterprising reporter should arrange an exclusive interview, where would it originate? Would television cameras have to be set up in heaven for such an interview? Or would it be a purgatory dateline? We would not want to consider hell as a possible point of origin.

Would our radio sets tune in far-away spirit voices and our television sets show filmy, elusive pictures from another sphere? Would we have to visit the séance, or the hypnotist—or even a flying-saucer club—to tune in? Or could it be that the interview could not be held at all, our Unknown Soldier having slipped quietly into the nothingness of oblivion?

Questions such as these—especially as they arise from the loss of our own loved ones—hover in the background of the mind during the entire lifetime. And they become more insistent with the passing years. Is there a satisfying answer?

These are the questions of the ages. Where are our beloved dead? Will they be returned to us? Is there something better beyond this day of difficult goodbyes?

17

There are various opinions—sincere opinions—as to the condition of man in death. Some say that if a good man dies, his soul goes immediately to heaven; that if a bad man dies, he goes at once to hellfire. Others say that this is not entirely true. They claim that when a man dies he stops over at a place called purgatory for cleansing.

Others insist that he goes to the spirit world where he is able to send messages to his loved ones. Still others tell us gloomily that when a man dies that is the end of him forever.

But there are many who sincerely believe that when a man dies he quietly sleeps until the resurrection day.

You can readily see that not all of these opinions can possibly be correct, for they are contradictory. And certainly a man who stands this side of death's door cannot of himself know what lies in and beyond the grave.

It is understandable, then, that there should be much confusion in this area. For death, unfortunately, simply cannot be subjected to test-tube experimentation.

I have investigated most of the theories of men regarding death and the hereafter. I have seen the attempts of theosophy to blend the major religions in an endeavor to find the answer. I have traveled in the East, with its mystic religions, and felt the fascination of their appeal.

A man does not soon forget the haunting hopelessness on the faces of mourners in the Hundu burning ghats of Calcutta or Bombay, for example. Or the confusion and despair among the mourners who have been taught to say, "There is no death."

I have witnessed with keenest interest the growth of the psychic sciences in both Europe and America during recent years, especially since the baptism of sorrow occasioned by global war—an opportunity of which spiritism has taken full advantage.

And then, I have studied the doctrines of the various churches, and talked with many people, and examined my own thinking. And I have been forced to the conclusion that in this area it is easy to step onto some mighty dangerous ground.

And so I keep coming back to the safest ground I know, the Word of the living God, with its simple questions and its logical answers.

One of the oldest questions ever asked is written in Job 14:14: "If a man die, shall he live again?" KJV.

And the apostle Paul, that intellectual genius of the Christian faith, puts the answer so plainly that none can fail to understand. "For if the dead rise not, then is not Christ raised: and if Christ be not raised, your faith is vain; ye are yet in your sins. Then they also which are fallen asleep in Christ are perished. If in this life only we have hope in Christ, we are of all men most miserable." 1 Corinthians 15:16-19, KJV.

Notice the clear, straight reasoning Paul uses here. He says that if we have hope only in this life, we are of all men most miserable. This life is not enough. It is not satisfactory even at its best.

Think it through for a moment. If all life amounts to is getting a start, building a home, becoming established, making a material success, achieving social distinction, but going down to the grave without hope of anything in the future—then are we not most miserable? The finest things in life have been left out.

When Jesus was here, He talked much and often about His Father's house. He urged His followers to look beyond this life, to look beyond the grave and death. And then, in one of the most profound and miraculous demonstrations of all time, He laid down His own life—and on the third day rose from the dead.

At that moment the power of death was broken. And now, for the first time in human history, there surged in man's breast the living conviction that his fondest hope, so long cherished, had at last been made certain. Our dead could be seen and loved again!

The prophet Isaiah, long centuries before, had written it. He had said, "Thy dead men shall live, together with my dead body shall they arise. . . . And the earth shall cast out the dead." Isaiah 26:19, KJV.

"Thy dead men shall live." Does not that mean, "Your dead, too, shall live"? Wonderful news!

Isaiah, looking down the long centuries, had declared it a certainty. But Jesus did more than that. He demonstrated it.

It is on this indisputable fact that the apostle Paul builds his strongest argument to bring hope to bereaved men and women down to the end of time. "For if the dead rise not, then is not Christ raised."

Let me ask you, Do you believe that Jesus rose from the dead? Of course you do, if you are a Christian. Then remember this. The resurrection of your loved one is as certain as the resurrection of Christ!

One of the most fascinating incidents coming from the annals of a past generation tells of the remarkable conversion of two great men who were avowed skeptics. One was the eminent Gilbert West; the other, Lord Lyttelton, the famous English jurist.

These two men agreed that Christianity should be destroyed. But they also agreed that to destroy it, two things were necessary. They must disprove the resurrection, and they must dispose of the conversion of the apostle Paul.

They divided the task between them, West assuming responsibility for the resurrection and Lyttelton caring for the experience on the Damascus road.

They were to give themselves plenty of time—a year or more, if necessary. But when they met again to compare notes, they had both become strong and devoted Christians, each testifying to the remarkable change in his life through contact with the risen Christ.

I have discovered that if anything will unsettle the skeptic, it will likely not be argument, however sane or sound. Rather, it will be the degree of personal conviction. And that conviction depends upon the reality of one's own commitment to a risen Lord.

Perhaps someone is saying, "I believe in the resurrection. But I am confused. What happens at death?"

Now at the risk of repetition, I must emphasize this basic scripture—the plainest text in all the Bible about what happens at death. It is found in Ecclesiastes 12:7: "Then shall the dust return to the earth as it was: and the spirit shall return unto God who gave it." KJV.

Here we have a description of what happens to a man when

he dies. But the question naturally arises, "What is this spirit that returns to God?"

The words of the apostle James may help us to understand. "For as the body without the spirit is dead, so faith without works is dead also." James 2:26, KJV. The spirit, then, is what keeps the body alive.

Have you ever noticed the notes down the center of the page in some Bibles? In these notes, opposite this text in James, you will discover that the word "spirit" may also be translated "breath." For the body without the *breath* is dead.

The two words "breath" and "spirit" are used interchangeably in Scripture. Job 27:3 says: "All the while my breath is in me, and the spirit of God is in my nostrils." KJV.

The spirit that a man receives from God and which goes back to God when he dies, is what God put into his nostrils. So we turn now to the record of man's creation. What did God put into man's nostrils?

"And the Lord God formed man of the dust of the ground, and breathed into his nostrils the breath of life; and man became a living soul." Genesis 2:7, KJV.

God breathed into man's nostrils at creation the breath of life. Then at death that spark or breath or spirit of life returns to God who gave it. It is the reverse of creation. Do you see?

"And the Lord God formed man of the dust of the ground." Shall we picture man as he came from the hands of his Creator? There he is—complete in every part. There is a brain in his head ready to think—but it isn't thinking. There is blood in his veins ready to flow—but it isn't flowing. There is a heart in his breast ready to beat—but it isn't beating. He is ready to live, to love, to act—but he isn't living, loving, or acting—yet.

Now listen. "And breathed into his nostrils the breath of life; and man became a living soul." From that moment man possessed an identity, a personality, a character. Man *became* a living soul as the result of the union of the body with the breath of life.

Then when a man dies, according to Ecclesiastes 12:7, the dust returns to the earth as it was, and the spirit of life, or breath of life, or spark of life, whether the man was saint or sinner, returns to God who gave it. The identity is not lost. The character is preserved. The personality is safe in the hands of God. But man is no longer conscious, because the life-giving, life-maintaining union of body and breath has been broken. Do you see?

In other words, if the union of the dust of the ground and the breath of life renders man a living soul, what happens to that soul when these two are separated at death? Anyone can see that man simply ceases to be a living soul until the Life-giver reunites the two on the morning of the resurrection.

In our last chapter we illustrated the important truth with an electric light bulb. Now may I illustrate it this way? Suppose that we have here a pile of boards and a pile of nails. That is all we have—just a pile of boards and a pile of nails. Now we take these boards and nail them together. We no longer have a pile of boards and a pile of nails—we now have a box.

Where did the box come from? "Oh," you say, "it didn't come from anywhere. It is simply the union of the pile of boards and the pile of nails." You are right.

Now let us suppose that we no longer want a box, so we pull out the nails and put them over here and place the boards back there. Now where did the box go? You say, "It didn't go any-where. It simply ceased to exist *as a box*." And you are right again. The boards still exist. The nails still exist. But there can be no box until the two are united again.

Just so, in the beginning, God formed man of two things—the dust of the ground, and the breath of life. As a result of the union of these two, man became a living, loving, acting soul. When he dies the two separate. The living, loving, acting soul—the combination of body and breath—doesn't go any-where. It simply surrenders its consciousness until the resur-rection morning when body and breath are united again. The Bible does not have a man nonexistent between death and the resurrection. It has him sleeping. That's Scripture, pure and simple!

Evidently, surprising as it may be to some, we do not go to our reward at death. Evidently death is simply a cessation of life until it is restored at the resurrection.

May I ask you to reason with me for a moment? You believe that there will be a resurrection at the last day. Of course you do. This has been one of the pillars of the Christian faith for centuries. In all the Scriptures it is held out as the only hope for the future.

But now let me ask you a question. Why would we need resurrection if, as some believe, we have already gone to the place of our reward at death? If we were enjoying the happiness of the home of the saved, would God return us to the grave so that we could be called forth in the resurrection?

Something is wrong here. And I fear that this inconsistency which crept into the Christian church centuries ago has caused countless men and women to lose confidence in the church.

Another question. Do you believe in the judgment at the last day? The Scripture says, "He hath appointed a day, in the which he will judge the world." Acts 17:31, KJV. But why would men need a judgment if they were rewarded at death? Are they not already judged?

And again. We believe that Jesus will return to this earth and that the avowed purpose of His coming is to receive His people. He said, "I will come again, and receive you unto myself; that where I am, there ye may be also." John 14:3, KJV.

Tell me. Do you make a trip to get your loved ones if you already have them with you? Why would Jesus need to come back and call His own from their graves if they were already with Him?

No. According to the Scriptures, death does not mean to go to heaven. Death does not mean to go to hellfire. Death does not mean to go to purgatory. Death does not mean to go to the spirit world. Death does not mean to go anywhere. Death simply means a cessation of life until the resurrection. Do you see?

Where, then, is our Unknown Soldier friend? According to the Scriptures, he is simply sleeping within his guarded tomb— unconscious of the honor heaped upon him—quietly waiting for the resurrection.

We do not go over the mystic river one by one. We all go together, at Christ's return. Listen!

"For the Lord himself shall descend from heaven with a

shout, with the voice of the archangel, and with the trump of God: and the dead in Christ shall rise first: then we which are alive and remain shall be caught up together with them in the clouds, to meet the Lord in the air: and so shall we ever be with the Lord." 1 Thessalonians 4:16, 17, KJV.

This is the promise. But this is still future.

Even Jesus called death a sleep. He said in John 11:11, "Our friend Lazarus sleepeth; but I go, that I may awake him out of sleep." KJV.

His disciples did not quite understand. They knew that Lazarus was ill, and suggested that if he were ill it might be better for him to sleep. "Then said his disciples, Lord, if he sleep, he shall do well. Howbeit Jesus spake of his death: but they thought that he had spoken of taking of rest in sleep. Then said Jesus unto them plainly, Lazarus is dead." KJV.

You remember the story. The sisters of Lazarus thought that Jesus had arrived too late. But He stood beside that tomb and cried, "Lazarus, come forth"! And Lazarus came forth. Someone has suggested that it is well that Jesus specified He was speaking only to Lazarus. Otherwise, every tomb on earth would have opened!

Lazarus came forth. Did Lazarus have a story to tell of his four days beyond death's door? Did Jesus call him back from the joys of a better life to resume his existence on this gloomy planet? No. Jesus simply called him forth from sleep—a sleep that can be broken only by the call of the Life-giver.

More than fifty times the Bible speaks of death as a sleep. Think it through with me. Is there anything more wonderful than dreamless, peaceful sleep at night? All toil, care, and heartache forgotten—no pain, no tears to moisten the eye. When we are asleep, you see, we have no sense of the passing of time.

Even so the Christian who dies, in one instant closes his eyes in the sleep of death, and to him it seems the next instant that he awakens in the resurrection to the joys of eternity. It will seem to him as though he had just had a short nap, even though he may have been in the grave many years. God's way is the best after all.

For doesn't that take the sting out of death? Think of it. The Christian may close his eyes in sleep for a hundred years perhaps; yet to him it will seem the very next moment when he opens his eyes to see Jesus. Only moments away from looking into the face of the Saviour. Is there any sting in that?

Does not this help us to understand the desire of Paul to "depart, and to be with Christ" and "to be absent from the body, and to be present with the Lord"? Some have been confused by his words, interpreting them to mean that he expected to be with Christ immediately at death. But did he? Listen to his triumphant words as he neared the end of life:

"For I am now ready to be offered, and the time of my departure is at hand. I have fought a good fight, I have finished my course, I have kept the faith: henceforth there is laid up for me a crown of righteousness, which the Lord, the righteous judge, shall give me *at that day*: and not to me only, but unto all them also that love *his appearing*." 2 Timothy 4:6-8, KJV.

The time of his departure, his death, was at hand. But when did he expect to receive his reward? *At that day*—along with all the saved. When did he expect to be with Christ? *At His appearing*. Paul was simply passing over the lapse of time, which would seem as a moment, to the day of the resurrection. That was his hope.

When a Christian dies, he can know that in that resurrection morning his life will not only be restored, but he will be given immortal life.

Here are the striking details. Listen! "Behold, I show you a mystery; We shall not all sleep, but we shall all be changed, in a moment, in the twinkling of an eye, at the last trump: for the trumpet shall sound, and the dead shall be raised incorruptible, and we shall be changed. For this corruptible must put on incorruption, and this mortal must put on immortality." 1 Corinthians 15:51-53, KJV.

Remember? "For the Lord himself shall descend from heaven with a shout, with the voice of the archangel, and with the trump of God: and the dead in Christ shall rise first: then we which are alive and remain shall be caught up together with them in the clouds, to meet the Lord in the air: and so shall we ever be with the Lord. Wherefore comfort one another with these words." 1 Thessalonians 4:16-18, KJV.

I ask you. Could there be any better news—any better comfort?

Picture it if you can. The Son of God piercing the vaulted heavens, moving down the star-studded procession way of the skies, attended by myriads of angels. And then He calls out with a voice of thunder, "Awake, ye that sleep in the dust of the earth. Arise to everlasting life." And *your dead, too,* will hear!

That voice calling our beloved dead will be heard the world around. Families will be reunited. Children snatched away by death will be placed again in their mothers' arms. What a glad reunion day!

What does this mean to you? What does it mean to me? It means that there is something better *beyond this day!*

Think for a moment. Think what that day will mean to the crippled, to the blind, to those weakened by disease, to minds confused by fear. God says, "The eyes of the blind shall be opened, and the ears of the deaf shall be unstopped. Then shall the lame man leap, . . . and the tongue of the dumb sing." Isaiah 35:5, 6, KJV.

But think what it will mean to the able-bodied and the strong, to those who love life and want to live. You see, death may even seem welcome to a body racked by disease and pain. But to the strong and youthful, death can mean only disappointed hopes, disillusionment, shattered ambitions.

But here is the answer to death's sting. Not in the discoveries of science, not in the exploration of outer space, not in anything man can do, but in the promise of the resurrection made by One who Himself demonstrated its possibility—here is our hope!

The Trail of Intrigue

The year was 1940. Hitler and his forces, in their blitz of terror, were pushing unchecked across the lowlands of Europe. The peace-loving people of the Netherlands came under Nazi rule. Invasion money was put into circulation.

And then a curious thing was noticed. The printing date, on this invasion money, was 1935! Five years before he took over the country, his plans all unsuspected, Hitler's presses were rolling off invasion money.

Shrewd preplanning!

I invite you now to trace with me a devious trail of intrigue beginning with war on another world, and involving the most subtle infiltration, the cleverest and most successful propaganda, the shrewdest preplanning on the part of a rebel general that this planet has ever known.

Watch, if you will, the subversion of a world!

We pick up the story (repeated, if you don't mind—for it is so important), I say we pick up the story as a beautiful woman stands fascinated beside a most interesting tree. Ringing in her ears are the words of the God of heaven, "In the day that thou eatest thereof thou shalt surely die." Genesis 2:17, KJV.

Suddenly a beautiful serpent, resting in the tree, begins to speak. He asks in the disguise of innocence, "Hath God said, Ye shall not eat of every tree of the garden?" Genesis 3:1, KJV.

And she replies, "We may eat of the fruit of the trees of the garden: but of the fruit of the tree which is in the midst of the garden, God hath said, Ye shall not eat of it, neither shall ye touch it, lest ye die."

Now watch. "And the serpent said unto the woman, *Ye shall not surely die.*"

Subtle, but direct, contradiction. "*Ye shall not surely die.*" And he continued, "For God doth know that in the day ye eat thereof, then your eyes shall be opened, and *ye shall be as gods,* knowing good and evil."

Here is the double line of propaganda that has echoed down through the ages to your ears and mine. "*Ye shall not surely die.*" And "*ye shall be as gods.*" It has never changed. We shall meet it again and again.

Who is this secret agent of rebellion who speaks through the serpent? Jesus says he fell from heaven. "I beheld Satan as lightening fall from heaven." Luke 10:18, KJV.

John in the Revelation gives more detail: "And there was war in heaven: Michael and his angels fought against the dragon; and the dragon fought and his angels, and prevailed not; neither was their place found anymore in heaven. And the great dragon was cast out, that old serpent, called the devil, and Satan, which deceiveth the whole world: he was cast out into the earth, and his angels were cast out with him." Revelation 12:7-9, KJV.

Are we dealing with a two-horned monster with red skin and a pitchfork? No. Such a caricature, carried over from the Dark Ages, has caused many a man to dismiss the whole idea of an evil personality with disgust.

Rather, we are dealing with an intelligent being who was once in heaven, and who fell from heaven. Isaiah names him:

"How art thou fallen from heaven, O Lucifer, son of the morning! how art thou cut down to the ground, which didst weaken the nations! For thou hast said in thine heart, I will ascend into heaven, I will exalt my throne above the stars of God: I will sit also upon the mount of the congregation, in the sides of the north: I will ascend above the heights of the clouds; I will be like the most High." Isaiah 14:12-14, KJV.

What a revelation! Lucifer, son of the morning, one of the most brilliant intellects in all the universe—this is Satan. This is the devil. This is the source of evil, the source of trouble. Ezekiel describes him:

"Thou hast been in Eden the garden of God; every precious stone was thy covering, the sardius, topaz, and the diamond, the beryl, the onyx, and the jasper, the sapphire, the emerald, and the carbuncle, and gold: the workmanship of thy tabrets and of thy pipes was prepared in thee in the day that thou wast created. Thou art the anointed cherub that covereth; and I have set thee so: thou wast upon the holy mountain of God; thou hast walked up and down in the midst of the stones of fire. Thou wast perfect in thy ways from the day that thou wast created, till iniquity was found in thee." Ezekiel 28:13-15, KJV.

Did God create a devil? Is He therefore responsible for evil? No. God created a perfect being who corrupted himself.

You see, God created all His beings with the power of choice. This majestic being was given the power of choice just as you and I have been given it.

God took a terrible chance when He made His creatures with the power to choose. Somebody, someone, might choose wrong. And Lucifer was that one. Pride corrupted this prince of angels.

Sin had entered a perfect universe. Something had to be done about it. God, in His wisdom, saw fit not to destroy sin immediately. Rather, the plant of sin must be allowed to develop, that all might judge its bloom.

In the meantime, there must come an open confrontation between the forces of good and evil. And so there was war in heaven. Satan and his angels were cast out.

The controversy moved to this earth, where it has raged ever since. Satan has been cast out of heaven, but he is determined to gain control of this planet in rebellion, and every man in it. What a drama! And you and I are the actors, while all the universe looks on.

The controversy isn't over yet. And what do we face?

"Therefore rejoice, ye heavens, and ye that dwell in them. Woe to the inhabiters of the earth and of the sea! for the devil is come down unto you, having great wrath, because he knoweth that he hath but a short time." Revelation 12:12, KJV.

This is what we face. An angry devil. Furious because his

time is short. And he is not only angry, but subtle.

But now back to Eden. Watch the enemy of God as he carefully lays his plans, as he chooses the line he will follow through the ages.

"*Ye shall not surely die.*" You are immortal. You cannot die. And "*ye shall be as gods.*" There is a spark of divinity within you. All you need to do is develop it. Such is the reasoning.

Do these words have a familiar ring to modern ears?

Is it not strange that nearly the entire Christian world sincerely believes that man was created immortal, not subject to death? Yet the only announcement of man's innate immortality in all the Scriptures comes from the devil himself—not from God. It was the rebel general who, shrewdly choosing his line, said, "*Ye shall not surely die.*"

In the record of man's creation there is nothing to intimate that man is immortal. "And the Lord God formed man of the dust of the ground, and breathed into his nostrils the breath of life; and man became a living soul." Genesis 2:7, KJV.

It is interesting to notice that if the breath of life, which made man a living soul, made him immortal, then the animals must also be immortal, for in Genesis 7:15 we read that "they went in unto Noah into the ark, two and two of all flesh, *wherein is the breath of life.*" KJV.

The truth is that the word "immortal" is used only once in the King James Version of the Bible. You will find it in 1 Timothy 1:17. But it refers to God. The word "immortality" is found five times in the King James Version. One of these references is 1 Timothy 6:16: "*Who only hath immortality*, dwelling in the light which no man can approach unto; whom no man hath seen, nor can see: to whom be honor and power everlasting." And verse 15 makes it clear that Paul is speaking of God. God, then, is the only One who has immortality.

Does this mean that even the angels are not immortal? We point out that Satan and his angels are to be destroyed. If they were created immortal, or imperishable, then God would not be able to destroy them.

Is man, then, without the hope of immortality? Far from it. But the Scriptures present it as a promise, not a present possession. We will be given immortality only if and when we have demonstrated that God can trust us with it. God promises life in obedience. It is His enemy who promises life in disobedience.

Trace with me the trail of intrigue. For this myth of man's natural immortality is the most widespread and persistent the world has ever known. Its continuity has never been broken. It spread from the gates of Eden to the pagan nations as they developed. And then spiritism in various forms began to dominate the worship of these peoples who knew not God. Belief in the persistence of the soul, the consciousness of the spirit after death, became an integral part of the pagan structure. Cults and incantations, necromancy and witchcraft, familiar spirits and diviners, all flourished in paganism.

Under Greece this concept of innate immortality reached its peak of development. From Greece it spread to the Jewish church in the last few centuries before Christ, and from Judaism, later, to the Christian churches in the early centuries. Then followed the long silence of the Dark Ages, and it was not until Reformation days that this false teaching was widely exposed. Martin Luther called it a monstrous fable.

The trail runs through all the Eastern religions. We find it in Hindu thought, in every Eastern cult, in theosophy, and penetrating deep into various Western adaptations. The doctrine of reincarnation is, of course, the doctrine of immortality in another guise.

It was in the nineteenth century that spiritualism erupted in the United States, beginning in 1848 with the "raps of Hydesville." These crude communications were at first largely considered as fraud and humbug. There were spirit rappings, mediums, séances, ouija boards, table tippings, and such.

But by 1893 spiritualism had shifted to a religious basis and called itself a church. Then after several decades in this form it took on a more "scientific" aspect, to match the tempo of the times. Says Alson J. Smith: "Psychical research rode into the camp of science on the coattails of psychology, and when it got there it changed its name to 'parapsychology' (a study of the phenomena that are beyond the present scope of psychology)."—*Immortality, the Scientific Evidence*, page 138.

And now, under laboratory control, psychic phenomena are supposedly weighed, measured, counted, dissected, and tabulated for the doubting mind.

It is a long and devious trail. But two features everywhere are evident: "*Ye shall not surely die.*" And "*ye shall be as gods.*" The shrewd rebel general presents his case in many forms, in many wrappings. But through the centuries his aims are clear as a bell. There is no death, he says. And there is a spark of divinity within you.

The authoritative *National Spiritualist Association Yearbook* (1961) says: "Spiritualism is God's message to mortals, declaring that There Is No Death. That all who have passed on still live. That there is hope in the life beyond for the most sinful.

"That every soul will progress through the ages to heights, sublime and glorious, where God Is Love and Love Is God."— Page 13.

No death! Immortality for all—even for the most sinful! But strange, is it not, that spiritualism labels itself a "message to *mortals*"? Did the truth slip out?

Think with me for a moment. What is the purpose of all this? Why did the rebel general lay his plans as he did? Why did he choose this particular propaganda line?

Does not a shrewd general look first to his communication lines? Can he hope to infiltrate peoples and nations without those lines? The enemy of God chose well his propaganda. For if the dead are still alive, then they can communicate with us. *And if men and women believe that the dead can communicate, the devil has an open line to the soul over which he can freely feed his suggestions of whatever nature!*

The churches in the mainstream of Christianity have long held themselves aloof from spiritualism. But spiritualism asks, "Why should you? You believe in immortality. We have proved it."

Will spiritualism yet be the means of uniting the Protestant and Catholic churches into one? There is that possibility. And if it happens, the common ground will be the belief in man's natural immortality, a concept completely foreign to sacred Scripture.

Now, I would not for a moment suggest that those who believe in innate immortality are knowing partners in a devilish scheme. The belief is held by millions of honest, sincere men and women who have never suspected its origin. In fact, that belief has so infiltrated the church that it is associated with some of our tenderest memories. Rarely is a loved one laid to rest without it. Some of our most beautiful concepts have come from it.

Never an Easter morning passes without eagerly reliving the experience of the thief on the cross and the assurance of Jesus that he would be with Him in Paradise that very day. They read, "And he said unto Jesus, Lord, remember me when thou comest into thy kingdom. And Jesus said unto him, Verily I say unto thee, Today thou shalt be with me in paradise." Luke 23:42, 43, KJV.

Yet little do preacher or congregation dream that here is an example of how popular thinking has influenced even the punctuation of the Scriptures. For the comma, you see, belongs *after* the word "today" rather than before it.

Never let a comma, misplaced by sincere men long centuries after Luke wrote his Gospel, confuse you. For how could either Christ or the thief have gone to Paradise that day? The Scripture narrative, when we examine it carefully, is quite revealing. The thief, no doubt, did not die that day. He did not expect to die that day. He did not expect Jesus to die that day. He knew that death by crucifixion was a long, slow process, often taking several days. You recall the surprise of Pilate, late that afternoon, when he learned that Jesus was already dead.

And death for the Son of God was to be like that which comes to every man—quiet, restful sleep. He was to be resurrected, not from three days in Paradise, but from three days in the tomb. He would say to Mary when He made Himself known on that Sunday morning, "Touch me not; for I am *not yet ascended* to my Father." John 20:17, KJV.

You see the problem. How could the thief possibly be with Christ in Paradise on Friday, as is commonly believed, if Christ Himself, on Sunday morning, stated positively that He had not yet ascended?

No, the thief knew when it would happen. He looked far past that dark hour when he said, "Remember me *when thou comest into thy kingdom.*" He looked far down the corridors of time to the day when He whose right it is to reign shall receive the kingdom from His Father. And Jesus, cheered by his faith, responded: I say unto you today, you will be with Me in Paradise.

I wonder if we realize the faith it took for the dying thief to pray that prayer. For if ever it appeared that He who called Himself the Son of God would have no kingdom, it was at that hour. And I wonder if we can comprehend the faith it took for the Son of God to answer as He did. Notice the vital significance of that word "today." *Today,* when even My own disciples have forsaken Me. *Today,* when My own people have crucified Me. *Today,* when it appears that I shall never have a kingdom. *Today,* when it looks as though I could never save anybody. I say unto you *today,* you will be with Me in Paradise.

Certainly, in the light of past teaching, much confusion, honest confusion, is inevitable. But we have come to a day when we must correctly understand this issue of immortality—or meet with fatal deception. It may mean laying aside a few cherished concepts. But the alternative is to be caught up in a delusion that will sweep the world. And when it does, not many will be spared!

Listen to this: "For they are the spirits of devils, working miracles, which go forth unto the kings of the earth and of the whole world, to gather them to the battle of that great day of God Almighty." Revelation 16:14, KJV.

This is what we can expect in earth's last hour. This is what you and I can expect to meet—in our day. Clever, subtle deceptions. Miracles, not tricks.

Oh, that we could write it in letters of fire—*not all miracles are necessarily from God!* It is only when men and women get hold of the fact that devils can work miracles and even in the name of Christ—it is only when we understand this important matter that we can be prepared for the crisis, for the deceptions that will sweep this old world in these last days.

But the average individual's understanding of this thing—or rather, his lack of understanding—is simply appalling!

It is incredible how superficial our reasoning can be when it involves the senses and the emotions. If a thing is supernatural, it must be from God. So we think. We see something. We feel something. We hear something. Somebody calls it a miracle. Perhaps it *is* a miracle. And just because it is beautiful, just because it is light, just because it is in the church, just because it is supernatural, we say it must be all right.

Nothing could be farther from the truth!

Do you remember Jesus' comment about the day of judgment? He said, "Not everyone that saith unto me, Lord, Lord, shall enter into the kingdom of heaven; but he that doeth the will of my Father which is in heaven. Many will say to me in that day, Lord, Lord, have we not prophesied in thy name? and in thy name have cast out devils? and in thy name done many wonderful works? And then will I profess unto them, I never knew you: depart from me, ye that work iniquity." Matthew 7:21-23, KJV.

Miracles in the church. Yes. But at least in some cases Christ will have nothing to do with them.

We say, I saw it with my eyes, I felt it with my feelings, I heard it with my ears.

I say it kindly. Wake up, friend! We are long past the time when we can depend upon our eyes, depend upon our ears, depend upon our feelings.

I say, we are living at a time when we cannot trust our senses. And the sooner we realize it the better. For the enemy's deceptions in these last days will not be clumsy. They will not be crude. They will be so subtle, so clever, so shrewdly adapted to a space-minded generation, that not a person will be safe unless his or her feet are solidly grounded on an "It is written."

In an hour like this shall we visit some teller of fortunes, cross her palm with silver, and commit our future to the drawing of a card? Shall we trust to luck or accident, to four-leaf clovers and rabbits' feet? Shall we turn to the crystal ball, in an hour like this?

Some have. Hitler in desperation summoned mediums and necromancers as his counselors. Shaw Desmond tells us that the same spirit consultation marked the tragedy of Mussolini.

Some of Kaiser Wilhelm's generals were known to have habitually consulted the spirits.

Two of our beloved presidents have, in days of crisis, called for psychic counsel. Should we too? One president is said to have had repeated contact with a medium. And another, shortly before his death, twice called to the White House a reader of the crystal ball.

Currently, the phenomenal Jeane Dixon, prophetess of Washington, who so accurately predicted the assassination of John F. Kennedy and certain other tragedies, is sought out repeatedly by diplomats of many nations.

Evidently we are not dealing with minor issues. And the tempo of the times demands serious evaluation of such phenomena. Predictions are being fulfilled. Much good is being done. Lives are being spared.

But are we to depend upon the crystal ball in an hour like this? Is the crystal ball the hope of mankind? Has the dramatic impact of the psychic reading, with its almost immediate fulfillment, taken the place of the stability of Scripture, the stately march of Bible prediction? Is God clothing His answers to man's frantic questions in the uncanny pictures of the crystal ball?

"I don't know whether I believe in Jeane Dixon or not," said one. "But I know one thing. If she told me not to get on a plane, I wouldn't."

Neither would I. For I strongly suspect that occult forces able to originate such uncannily correct predictions are well able to crash a plane.

Predictions. Correct predictions. Plane crashes. Suicides. Business deals. Marriages. Elections. Personal decisions. But I ask, Is God to become nothing more than a dependable reservation agency for safe air travel? Where are the broad lines of prophecy that affect all humanity?

I keep thinking of the words of Deuteronomy 13:1-3. Listen:

"If there arise among you a prophet, or a dreamer of dreams, and giveth thee a sign or a wonder, and the sign or the wonder come to pass, whereof he spake unto thee, saying, Let us go after other gods, which thou hast not known, and let us serve them; thou shalt not hearken unto the words of that prophet, or that dreamer of dreams: for the Lord your God proveth you, to know whether ye love the Lord your God with all your heart and with all your soul."

Here is described a situation where a prophet makes predictions. And the predictions come true. But the teaching of the prophet does not harmonize with the Word of God. We are not to follow that prophet, regardless of the accuracy of prediction. The God of heaven is only proving His people.

Said the prophet Isaiah: "To the law and to the testimony: if they speak not according to this word, it is because there is no light in them." Isaiah 8:20, KJV.

Error, sooner or later, shows the telltale signs of its origin. When a modern prophet recounts a vision in which she is led by a serpent to look to the East for wisdom—that breeding ground of false teaching—I begin to wonder.

And when she predicts that a child born under the symbol of sun worship—age-long enemy of the worship of God—is one day to become the savior of mankind, I wonder even more!

The trail of intrigue is enchanted ground. From Eden to Armageddon, from the serpent to the crystal ball, it is dangerous ground!

Look to the East for wisdom? I urge you rather—look to the Book!

Psychic Cinerama

And so a bewildered generation finds itself, without choosing, inescapably involved in a psychic cinerama, surrounded as by a giant circular screen. The picture boldly invades the consciousness of man, tracing persistent images difficult to erase. Its sounds bombard us from every side. Its action rushes toward us as if we ourselves were a moving camera. No longer the weird, the crude, the eerie. Today it is the subtle, the clever, the seemingly innocent fascination of the unknown world.

You and I are caught in the center of a bewildering psychic drama the like of which the world has never known. And if we are wise enough not to trust our senses, we shall escape!

Death, from the day it first coldly introduced itself to man, has been a forbidding enigma. But it has been reserved for this generation to probe deeper into the mystery of life and death than any other. This is a generation that crowds eternity—and wants to know what is there!

It is little wonder, then, that this questioning generation finds itself surrounded by a psychic cinerama that defies description. No man can close his eyes to it. It is there. He can see it, hear it, feel it. Every man must decide what his relationship to it shall be.

Do those who turn to psychic phenomena find the answers? Are the voices they hear out of the silence the voices of the dead? Can we reach out into another world with our fingertips? And if we can, is it safe to do so?

Here we meet an issue that comes very close to the human heart. For who can fail to understand the loneliness, the silence, that settles down upon one who has seen some treasured life slip into the shadows of death? Yesterday life was complete. Doors were open. Goodbyes were followed by reunion. But today life has broken in two. Doors have slammed shut. And it all seems so final. No wonder the lonely heart seeks comfort from whatever source.

The awful carnage and baptism of sorrow occasioned by global war have given to psychic cults an opportunity of which they have taken full advantage. Countless thousands are turning to these movements—some in the spirit of scientific investigation, others out of curiosity or for entertainment. And the number is legion who in their desperate loneliness have become confirmed devotees.

Psychic research has put on its laboratory coat and crept into our universities. It is tugging at the edges of the medical profession. The hypnotist is attempting to probe deeper into the secrets of life. Telepathy and clairvoyance, precognition and psychokinesis and the crystal ball—these have become a part of the everyday conversation of serious-minded men.

You may, however, be one of the many who have cast all psychic phenomena aside as trickery. You may have dismissed it from your mind as fraud. But while some of it may be trickery —and even its own adherents admit that within the psychic circle there is much fraud—yet the person who dismisses it all as trickery or fraud has not had the slightest glimpse into these movements which had their origin in ancient times and which have left indelible marks on all the centuries, until today no man or woman can be oblivious to their impact.

I visited recently in the home of a physician in a midwestern city. This gracious gentleman was at that time a confirmed devotee of the Eastern cults, a firm believer in reincarnation. In fact, he had in his study a shelf five feet wide filled with recorded tapes supposedly delineating the details of previous lives of himself and his wife.

Yet this man did not sense any contradiction in belonging to one of the largest Christian churches in the nation. After all, the church taught that the soul is immortal. Why should he not believe in reincarnation?

And his reasoning was not inconsistent. For if a man believes in innate immortality, why rule out the Eastern cults? If the dead are alive and able to communicate, why rule out psychic phenomena? What barrier is there against spiritism? What barrier is there against the orgies of voodoo? What barrier is there against the wildest incantations of the heathen world? Every barrier falls flat.

It is only when we learn the true origin of the doctrine of man's natural immortality that we sense the serious implications of involvement in the occult. It is only then that we hear the alarm bell.

Personally I am not a spiritualist or a psychic reader. I am not a follower of parapsychology or of the Eastern cults. I am not a hypnotist or a devotee of the crystal ball. I am not any of these—not because I doubt the phenomena, but because I have learned of their origin and mechanism as described in the Word of God.

The Scripture teaching on this popular subject is both adequate and clear—too clear to be misunderstood. Is it not both logical and wise that we should now examine it?

You see, we have come to a time when we dare not trust our five senses. Issues can no longer be safely decided by our eyes and our ears, much less our feelings. Some revelation from God is needed to guide the sincere seeker for truth.

But first, do we have clearly in mind just what we need to discover? The reason that most psychic cults have appealed to so many people is that they claim to give opportunity to heartsick, lonely, bereaved men and women to communicate with those they have lost. And it is the promise of communication with the wise who have passed on that creates the powerful temptation for world leaders to seek supernatural direction. Basically the psychic movements are all built upon the concept that the dead are not dead and are therefore able to communicate. This is what leads men and women to try to break the spirit barriers. This is what lures them to pound on the door of the unseen.

Now, this claim that the dead can communicate is either true or untrue. If true, it would be one of the grandest and sweetest truths that ever came to mourning humanity. If untrue, it is a shameless fraud perpetrated in the name of life's tenderest memories. As we open the Word of God, I leave it with you to decide. The claim is true or untrue. You will agree that it cannot be both.

Let me take you, then, to the one dependable source of information.

"And when they shall say unto you, Seek unto them that have familiar spirits, and unto wizards that peep, and that mutter: should not a people seek unto their God? for the living to the dead? To the law and to the testimony; if they speak not according to this word, it is because there is no light in them." Isaiah 8:19, 20, KJV.

Right on the subject, isn't it? But notice this scripture—verse 19—as translated by Dr. Moffatt: "When they tell you to consult mediums and ghosts that cheep and gibber in low murmers, ask them if a nation should not rather consult its God. Say, 'Why consult the dead on behalf of the living? Consult the message and counsel of God!' "

That is a straight, clear word from God. When we are invited to consult one who is sensitive in the psychic arts, one who claims contact with those departed, we should answer, "Why consult the dead on behalf of the living?" Rather, "Consult the message and the counsel of God."

Now, what does the message of God reveal about the dead? Do the dead come back?

"As the cloud is consumed and vanisheth away: so he that goeth down to the grave shall come up no more. He shall return no more to his house, neither shall his place know him anymore." Job 7:9, 10, KJV.

Evidently the dead do not come back.

Now follow me carefully. The great hope which the Scriptures hold out to the human heart is that on the resurrection morning—not at death—loved ones torn from us will be united with us again. In fact, the entire structure of Christianity rests upon the resurrection of Jesus Christ from the dead and the final resurrection of His followers in the last day. Job himself said, "For I know that my Redeemer liveth, and that he shall stand at the latter day upon the earth." Job 19:25, KJV. And he adds this triumphant note: "Yet in my flesh shall I see God." Verse 26.

But as to the dead coming out at the bidding of the curious or returning to their household to see how loved ones are getting along, the Word says, "He shall return no more to his house." The dead are not to be recalled until that grand and final day when Jesus himself shall return. In that day, and not until that day, death will give way to immortality, to eternal life.

The Scriptures go still farther. They say that at death man's power to think ceases. "Put not your trust in princes, nor in the son of man, in whom there is no help. His breath goeth forth, he returneth to his earth; in that very day his thoughts perish." Psalm 146:3, 4, KJV.

There need be no mistake here. The Creator knows what happens at death. And He tells us that the dead do not think. Let me read another scripture—perhaps the most important one that we shall read:

"For the living know that they shall die: but the dead know not anything. . . . Also their love, and their hatred, and their envy, is now perished." Ecclesiastes 9:5, 6, KJV.

There we have it! The dead know nothing. They cannot remember. They cannot love or hate or envy. Should not this forever settle the matter of what happens at death? "The dead know not anything."

However much you or I may have probed the mysteries of life and death and of the human mind, we do not know what is on the other side of the grave, except as the Word of God reveals it to us. But thank God, enough is revealed to inspire genuine hope within the human breast—hope that all humanity desperately needs. Jesus Himself said that our beloved dead rest peacefully until the resurrection day, and that then He will call them forth. "Marvel not at this: for the hour is coming, in the which all that are in the graves shall hear his voice, and shall come forth; they that have done good, unto the resurrection of life; and they that have done evil, unto the resurrection of damnation." John 5:28, 29, KJV.

Here the Creator of heaven and earth, who holds the issues of life and death in His hands, states simply that there is an hour coming when all the dead will hear His penetrating, life-giving voice. And then, not at death but on the resurrection morning, God's waiting ones will come forth with the priceless gift of immortality. That is the gospel, pure and simple!

Yes, one of the sweetest and most comforting truths in all of God's Book is that when a man dies he rests quietly, undisturbed by memories of a troubled life or by concern for his loved ones, until the promised resurrection day. One prominent businessman remarked, as he studied the Word of God on this subject, "If that isn't the way it is, then that's the way it ought to be!"

Did I say that we might have to lay aside a few cherished concepts when we learn the truth? Yes, our misunderstandings may have held a trace of beauty. But we see now that they are marred by fear and inconsistency. We lay them aside only to accept truth that is infinitely more satisfying. God's way is best. God's way offers the only lasting comfort. God's way is the truly beautiful.

Notice how consistent God's plan is. Think it through again. Why would we need a resurrection at the end of time if men go to their reward immediately at death? Why would Jesus need to return to this earth a second time, as He has promised, to gather His people, if they are already with Him in Paradise? Why do the Scriptures teach a judgment in the last days if men are already judged at death?

Do you see? The dead do not return to their houses. Their power to think ceases. They know nothing of the troubles of this earth. They rest, quietly, undisturbed, until Jesus calls them forth to everlasting life in that glorious reunion day.

An intelligent lady was studying the Bible on this subject. She had been very much interested in communication with the dead. But when she came to this particular point in her study, she exclaimed, "*Then who is writing on my slate?*"

Do you see her dilemma? If what we have read from the Scriptures is true—and it is—then who gives the messages in the darkened room? Who is masquerading in the disguise of those loved and lost?

These are the questions that are tapping insistently at inquiring minds. Who is writing on the slate? Who is reading the cards? Who is moving the pencil? Who is forming the pictures in the crystal ball? Who is so perfectly impersonating the voice of a lost loved one?

Prominent theologians, beloved leaders, trusted counselors describe sincerely and unashamedly their supposed contacts with relatives who have passed on. They wield tremendous influence over millions. Can it be that even giant intellects are deceived?

What are the powers that are unquestionably operating in the psychic world? We have seen what they are not. Then what are they? Who are they?

God tells us who the real powers are. The Scriptures identify those powers that parade in the garb of others as the followers of Lucifer, the fallen angels. And keep in mind that angels are not the spirits of the dead. Angels existed before this world was created, before ever a man had died.

I fully realize how difficult it is to grasp the idea that evil angels can actually work miracles. But that fact, I sincerely believe, is the key to understanding the psychic phenomena with which we are bombarded today. Please forever settle one thing in your mind. The supernatural, the miraculous, does not necessarily come from God! When that fact is fully established in your thinking, you are safeguarded from many a deception.

"For they are the spirits of devils, working miracles." Revelation 16:14, KJV.

You see, the fallen angels, the followers of Lucifer, the devils the Bible talks about, are superior intelligences. They can work miracles—miracles which will deceive all who are not guarded by a knowledge of Scripture. Satan can actually transform himself into an angel of light. "For such are false apostles, deceitful workers, transforming themselves into the apostles of Christ. And no marvel; for Satan himself is transformed into an angel of light." 2 Corinthians 11:13, 14, KJV.

You understand now that it is altogether possible for a fallen angel to masquerade as another being, to actually transform himself into the form of a loved one. With the intelligence of angels, and with thousands of years of experience, they are masters of impersonation. Nor do they lack information. Assigned to observe a family through the years, is it any wonder that they know Grandfather's voice, and how Aunt Susan arranged her hair, and where Uncle Ezra hid his will?

You begin to understand now what really happened in the experience of King Saul, in the séance described in the Bible. The account is found in 1 Samuel 28. Notice verses 6 and 7, KJV:

"And when Saul inquired of the Lord, the Lord answered him not, neither by dreams, nor by Urim, nor by prophets. Then said Saul unto his servants, Seek me a woman that hath a familiar spirit, that I may go to her, and inquire of her. And his servants said to him, Behold, there is a woman that hath a familiar spirit at Endor."

You have the setting. The Lord had refused to answer Saul. Samuel the prophet was dead. Saul went to the witch at Endor—a practice forbidden by God—and asked that Samuel be brought up. A form appeared having the likeness of Samuel. And then there is recorded a conversation supposedly between Saul and the prophet.

Did not Saul actually speak to Samuel? I ask you, How could he speak to Samuel if Samuel, like all the dead, was quietly resting in his grave with no knowledge of what was taking place? And would God send a message to Saul through the dead when He had already refused to communicate with him through His appointed means? You can see that the two sources of information are direct opposites.

No, the apparition claiming to be Samuel was not he. It was only an evil intelligence playing the part of Samuel in a psychic drama forbidden by God. And Saul died for his transgression. "So Saul died for his transgression which he committed against the Lord, even against the word of the Lord, which he kept not, and also for asking counsel of one that had a familiar spirit, to inquire of it." 1 Chronicles 10:13, KJV.

Saul died for his sin—as have many others since. For God

writes over the séance, over every attempt to contact the dead, "Wrong, wrong, wrong!"

The same evil powers that operated back there are operating today. Let me read it from the words of a spiritualist, F. F. Morse. In his book *Practical Occultism*, page 85, he says, "The phenomenal aspect of modern spiritualism reproduces all of the essential principles of the magic witchcraft and sorcery of the past. The same powers are involved, the same intelligences operating."

Revealing evidence, isn't it?

Let me say it as kindly and as earnestly as I know how. According to the Word of God these spirits which come to us and claim to be the dear ones taken away by death, are not dead people. They are not living people. They are not people at all! They are fallen angels masquerading in the form of our loved ones!

If we let our eyes decide it, who is it? Our loved one. If we let our ears decide it, who is it? Our loved one. If we let our feelings decide it, who is it? Our loved one. But if we let the Word of God decide it, who is it? *A masquerading impostor!*

I want to be kind. How could I have anything but understanding for those who have been sincere in their attempt to find comfort in the realm of the psychic? But the powers behind these phenomena take unfair advantage of men and women. They come with caresses and words of love when we are weak and sorrowful. That is why I feel compelled to speak as I do.

I have personally watched the growth of the psychic sciences in Asia and Europe and America. I have followed carefully the experiments in parapsychology at Duke University, as scientists with laboratory exactness have attempted to discover just what the extrasensory perception of the human mind might be. I have examined the cults of the dead, the accounts of the avatars of the East and their long trail of followers. I have visited the world seat of theosophy in Madras, India, and then seen the Eastern philosophies penetrating into the West under a multitude of unsuspected labels.

And I have found what many honest investigators have found before me. Sherwood Eddy, for instance, though greatly impressed with what he saw, confessed: "I frankly admit that there is not only triviality and contradiction but fraud and trickery in the psychic field."

Even Williams James likened some psychic research to "dredging in a dirty sea."

Please do not be confused. God's message for this critical hour is simply not found in the trivial disclosures of sometimes truthful and sometimes lying spirits. Saving truth is not contained in the "profound" information that two sisters had a ring, or in the materialization of an ash tray, or in the marvelous ability to see a table fork when someone else thinks about one.

"Have you seen Jesus?" one of the spirits was asked. And the spirit replied, "I have not seen Jesus over here, nor have I met any who have."

Jesus is not in spiritualism. There may be hymns in its séances, it may accept Him as a great medium. But He must leave the cross behind. Said Sir Arthur Conan Doyle, an outstanding devotee, "Spiritualism will sweep the world and make it a better place in which to live. When it rules over the world, it will banish the blood of Christ."

But any supposed hope for the world that leaves out the blood of Christ is an empty hope, a cold hope. Again I quote from Sherwood Eddy: "One sometimes feels in such writings the pantheistic chill of the arctic night."

No, man's hope is not in psychic phenomena, not in messages from a cold, filmy spirit land, not in the dead at all, but in the living Christ! Man shall not live by word from the dead, "but by every word that proceedeth out of the mouth of God." And His Word contains the most comforting promise ever made to suffering humanity: "I will come again, and receive you unto myself; that where I am, there ye may be also."

Seeing our Lord face to face. Joining our loved ones in the glorious light of never-ending day, nevermore to part. This is the promise! This is the gospel! This is the future that Calvary has made possible!

I urge you to turn aside every other consideration. Crowd out every other thought, and turn your eyes on Calvary. There is a controversy raging between good and evil, between right and wrong. Your only safety, my only safety, is to stand in the shadow of the cross!

> Beneath the cross of Jesus
>   I fain would take my stand,
> The shadow of a mighty rock
>   Within a weary land.

Will you stand with me there? There is no safer place in the all the world!

Cosmic Invasion

It was in 1898 that H. G. Wells's *The War of the Worlds* was published. It still stands as one of the most vivid pieces of imaginary writing ever put together. Long before the days of mechanized warfare, he wrote of fighting machines a hundred feet high, each manned by a Martian. He wrote of the heat ray, of gas warfare, the use of aircraft in battle. He wrote of remote-controlled handling machines that bear an uncanny resemblance to robots now being developed for use in the unfamiliar terrain of the moon. And H. G. Wells wrote it all in the first-person, straightforward, plotless style of a reporter just come from the scene.

It was on October 30, 1938, that a radio adaptation of *The War of the Worlds*, produced by Orson Welles, was presented over CBS radio. It was introduced as a dramatization, but was presented in the form of an actual newscast. And thousands who missed the opening announcement thought that an invasion from Mars was actually taking place. The result was panic over a large part of the eastern United States.

Can anyone doubt that today, conditioned as we are by space-age thinking, a presentation of *The War of the Worlds* would produce panic far more widespread than in 1938—if it were permitted on the air? For today a possible invasion from Mars, or somewhere else in space, has pushed outside the bounds of science fiction into serious discussion.

Is such a cosmic invasion a possibility? Can we know?

The truth is that the dependable Volume describes, not far in

51

the future, a cosmic invasion of this planet on a far greater scale than H. G. Wells ever dreamed, but far different.

For a moment watch with me a moving drama from the early days of World War II. It happened in the Philippines. General Douglas MacArthur had decided that in order to successfully wrest these great islands from the hand of a then-ruthless enemy, he must delay direction action. Under cover of darkness, and surrounded with but a few close aides, he left with the promise, "I will return!"

Not only an island, but the entire free world—and the free world's prestige and honor—was at stake. Millions hung on those words, "I will return!"

Reminiscent, isn't it, of another drama of deliverance even more vitally affecting you and me. Jesus, the Son of God, nineteen hundred years ago was preparing to leave this planet. He had laid careful plans to wrest this world—only a tiny island in the universe—from the hands of the enemy. But He must delay direct action. Quietly, and surrounded by a few friends, He had made that familiar promise, "I will return!" "I will come again!"

"Let not your heart be troubled: ye believe in God, believe also in me. In my Father's house are many mansions: if it were not so, I would have told you. I go to prepare a place for you. And if I go and prepare a place for you, I will come again, and receive you unto myself; that where I am, there ye may be also." John 14:1-3, KJV.

"I will return!" said MacArthur. "I will return!" said Jesus nineteen hundred years before him. And then, that day on Olivet, watch the moving scene: "And while they looked steadfastly toward heaven as he went up, behold, two men stood by them in white apparel; which also said, Ye men of Galilee, why stand ye gazing up into heaven? this same Jesus, which is taken up from you into heaven, shall so come in like manner as ye have seen him go into heaven." Acts 1:10, 11, KJV.

This same Jesus, with whom they had lived side by side, this same Jesus, who had endeared Himself to them by unforgettable acts of ministry, was to return. His every act, His every word, had brought these men to love Him as a person. And now this same Jesus would come again—as a person. Nothing less could give them hope.

Men will actually see Him come. "Behold, he cometh with clouds; and every eye shall see him." Revelation 1:7, KJV. Eyes of love, eyes of hate, eyes of scoffing, eyes of anticipation, eyes of weeping, eyes of gladness—*every eye* shall see Him come. "For as the lightning cometh out of the east, and shineth even unto the west; so shall also the coming of the Son of man be." Matthew 24:27, KJV.

Like a blaze of glory stretched from sky to sky, our Saviour will return to earth past constellations of unnumbered worlds. He will come, not as a Babe in Bethlehem, not as One despised and rejected of men, not condemned to die on a cross, but as King of kings and Lord of lords, whose right it is to reign!

He comes again, Creator of the speeding spheres. He returns a Conqueror, accompanied by all the angels of heaven. "When the Son of man shall come in his glory, and all the holy angels with him, then shall he sit upon the throne of his glory." Matthew 25:31, KJV.

How many angels are there? Revelation 5:11 tells us: "And I beheld, and I heard the voice of many angels round about the throne and the beasts and the elders: and the number of them was ten thousand times ten thousand and thousands of thousands."

What an invasion it will be! Bursting asunder the constellations, down the pathway of the skies, He comes to keep His promise to sorrowing humanity: "Let not your heart be troubled. . . . I will come again."

Some reverent astronomers have concluded that when our Lord returns, the vast corridor of Orion might be the star-lined processionway through which He will pass. Could this be true?

The Great Nebula in Orion, to the naked eye, appears as only a single hazy star. But the one-hundred-inch and the two-hundred-inch telescopes reveal this mystery of the heavens to be a tremendous cavern perhaps nineteen trillion miles across. Said the astronomer Larkin: "These negatives reveal the opening and interior of a cavern so stupendous that our entire solar system . . . would be lost therein."

And Garrett P. Serviss adds, "Is there not some vast mystery concealed in that part of the heavens? To me at least it seems so; for I can never shake off the impression that the creative power which made the universe lavished its richest gifts upon the locality in and surrounding Orion."

And what could Lord Tennyson have meant when, referring to Orion, he said, "I never gazed upon it but I dreamt of some vast charm concluded in that star to make fame nothing"?

One says, "Some vast mystery." Another says, "Some vast charm . . . to make fame nothing." What giant lodestone seems to be pulling minds to that part of the heavens? Could this canyon in the skies possibly be the corridor through which our Saviour will return? Many devout men think so!

But whatever His pathway, whatever vaulted highway of the sky our returning Lord might choose, the apostle Paul describes His descent in these positive, thrilling words: "For the Lord himself shall descend from heaven with a shout, with the voice of the archangel, and with the trump of God: and the dead in Christ shall rise first: then we which are alive and remain shall be caught up together with them in the clouds, to meet the Lord in the air: and so shall we ever be with the Lord." 1 Thessalonians 4:16, 17, KJV.

Streaming through the vaulted heavens, returning triumphantly to this wayward planet—what a picture it will be! Filling the skies with glory, He moves close to the earth, and then calls out—this time not to Lazarus alone, but to all His own who rest in the graves, "Come forth!" And they come forth!

This is when it happens. This is when our loved ones meet their Lord—not one by one at death, but all together, as the Son of God calls them forth.

Christ has not forgotten those who sleep. He gives them first attention. He calls them forth first—and then lifts them into the skies together with the living who are ready to meet Him.

It is then—at that glorious moment—that immortality is at last bestowed. In the twinkling of an eye the promise so long awaited is fulfilled. Paul describes that dramatic moment:

"Behold, I show you a mystery; We shall not all sleep, but we shall all be changed, in a moment, in the twinkling of an eye, at the last trump: for the trumpet shall sound, and the dead shall be raised incorruptible, and we shall be changed. For this corruptible must put on incorruption, and this mortal must put on immortality. So when this corruptible shall have put on incorruption, and this mortal shall have put on immortality, then shall be brought to pass the saying that is written, Death is swallowed up in victory. O death, where is thy sting? O grave, where is thy victory?" 1 Corinthians 15:51-55, KJV.

"This mortal must put on immortality." Man does not have it now. He puts it on, accepts it, receives it at that moment. This is the moment for which every Christian waits. This is the hope for immortality—not in the innovations of science, not in space travel, not in anything man can do, but in the promise of our Lord.

What will it be to see Jesus! Think what it will mean to those who have loved and lost. Think what it will mean to those long separated. Think what it will mean to those who gave their lives for their Lord. Think what it will mean to those who have waited for Him while the world scoffed. Think what it will mean to those who refused to follow the evidence of their senses, who refused to bow down to a masquerading impostor. And now their faith is rewarded. Their Lord has come. What will it be to see Jesus!

But someone is saying, "This is all so wonderful. But this is not for me. You see, my son, my daughter, was not a Christian."

I ask you, How do you know? How do you know?

I think of a mother who did her best to train her boy in the ways of right. But he turned out to be a criminal. And at last he was executed for his crime. His was one of three crosses on a hill outside Jerusalem.

His mother may have stood by weeping, her sobs caught up in the noise of the crowd. She may not have heard her son's words as he turned in those last moments to the one dying at his side and said, "Lord, remember me when thou comest into thy kingdom." I say, she may never have known.

Don't be too sure, then, that someone dear to you is lost. You, too, can turn to the Scriptures and share in their comfort and hope. Read the majestic words again:

"For the Lord himself shall descend from heaven with a shout, with the voice of the archangel, and with the trump of God: and the dead in Christ shall rise first: then we which are alive and remain shall be caught up together with them in the clouds, to meet the Lord in the air: and so shall we ever be with the Lord. Wherefore comfort one another with these words." 1 Thessalonians 4:16-18, KJV.

Could there be any better comfort?

There is something better beyond this day. Jesus is about to return. This symphony of tears will soon be over. What a day it will be!

I like to try to picture it. A small black cloud in the distance—drawing nearer and nearer—becoming lighter and more glorious—a great white cloud—its base like consuming fire—above it a rainbow. Jesus riding forth a mighty Conqueror. Not now a Man of Sorrows. Not now a crown of thorns. He comes as King of kings. And "the armies which were in heaven" follow Him. See Revelation 19:11-16. The vast, unnumbered throng of angels attend Him. The firmament seems filled with radiant forms.

What an invasion! No pen can portray it. No mortal mind can conceive its splendor. The Prince of life rides forth surrounded by a glory brighter than a thousand suns. The King of kings moves near the earth, wrapped in flaming light, looks upon the graves of the sleeping saints, and calls out, "Awake, awake, awake, ye that sleep in the dust, and arise!"

The whole earth rings with the tread of the army that comes forth from the prison house of death. And then, in a moment—in the twinkling of an eye—immortality at last!

And that day, friend, is not far off!

When the prophecies of Matthew 24 are fast fulfilling—*will He wait for long?*

When the inventions of men threaten to destroy the earth—*will He wait for long?*

When the enemy of God has concentrated all his efforts for one last battle—*will He wait for long?*

When the gong of doom is about to strike—*will He wait for long?*

A dark picture ahead? Atomic night? No, a glorious dawn, when the Prince of heaven, the King of kings, your Saviour and mine, shall return according to His promise to bring deliverance. Said the angel to Daniel, "And at that time thy people shall be delivered, everyone that shall be found written in the book." Daniel 12:1, KJV. Add to this the words of our Saviour, "Then look up; . . . for your redemption draweth nigh." Luke 21:28, KJV.

At that time—look up! Deliverance will come—from the skies!

May I take you back to that glad day at the close of the second world conflict when 2,000 prisoners of war in one camp were delivered from enemy hands? Two of the prisoners had built a little radio and secretly listened to the news. One day they heard a familiar voice. "This is General MacArthur speaking. I have returned!"

What marvelous news! The months had dragged wearily into two and a half long years since the day the general left behind him the promise to return. Now he was returning amid a thunder of guns, with an armada of ships and an air force the like of which had never before been seen in the Pacific.

In the meantime, the news filtered through the camp that the enemy, sensing the hopelessness of its own situation, and possibly in the spirit of reprisal, had actually decreed the death of the prisoners.

Among the prisoners was one who had been asked to serve as a camp official. One evening the guard informed him that at seven o'clock the next morning he was to call the prisoners together. Could this be the time when they would hear the long-feared death sentence?

Terrible were those hours as he watched the hands of the clock moving toward that fateful moment. Then he went out with the bell ringer to call the camp. The steel bar was raised, ready to strike the gong. Would this be the camp's death call?

But suddenly they both looked up. Each saw the same thing. In unison they exclaimed, "Look! Planes!" But were they friendly or enemy planes? The bell ringer, his hand still in the air, watched in breathless anticipation. Nearer and nearer they came. No, they were not enemy planes. As they roared over-head, paratroopers leaped out into the prison yards. Deliver-ance had come at last!

Make no mistake about it. The forces of evil are intent on destroying the human race. The enemy of God and man has his hand raised, ready to strike the death gong. The great contro-versy between Christ and Satan, between good and evil, be-tween right and wrong, is on the verge of its last titanic strug-gle. But *it is written,* "At that time thy people shall be deliv-ered." At that time—"look up; . . . for your redemption draweth nigh."

Down the minster aisles of splendor, from betwixt
    the cherubim,
  Through the wondering throng, with motion strong and fleet,
Sounds His victor tread approaching, with a music
    far and dim—
  The music of the coming of His feet.

Sandaled not with sheen of silver, girded not with woven gold,
  Weighted not with shimmering gems and odors sweet,
But white-winged and shod with glory in the Tabor light
    of old—
  The glory of the coming of His feet.

He is coming, O my friend, with His everlasting peace,
  With His blessedness immortal and complete;
He is coming, O my friend, and His coming brings release—
  I listen for the coming of His feet.

—Lyman Allen.

Footsteps in the sky! Deliverance at last! The Saviour face to face! Eternal life with Him!

Just think of taking hold of a hand and finding it God's hand! Just think of feeling invigorated and finding it immortality! Just think of waking up and finding home!

Firefall

It is nine o'clock on a summer evening in Yosemite National Park. There is an atmosphere of expectancy. Every eye is turned toward Glacier Point far above. And then, precisely at the stroke of nine, a voice rings out across the waiting camp, "Let the fire fall!"

And three thousand feet above the floor of the valley, a voice answers, "The fire falls!"

Flaming embers are pushed over the precipice, into the darkness of the summer night, and come cascading down the sheer white granite of the mountain wall. It is the famous firefall of Yosemite.

There will come a day when the voice of God will call out, "Let the fire fall!" And like a million firefalls, flames will cascade down the skies upon an unrepenting planet. And in that day, for every man who has rejected the Saviour, there will be no place to hide!

That firefall of the ages, that finish of the history of rebellion, will be what the prophet Isaiah calls God's "strange work; . . . His strange act." Isaiah 28:21, KJV.

A *strange act* for one who taught men to love their enemies! A *strange act* for one who refused to let His disciples call down fire upon those who slighted Him! A *strange act* for one who healed the ear of a man who had come to take His life! A *strange act* for one who prayed while they crucified Him, "Father, forgive them; for they know not what they do."

I fear that a misunderstanding of this strange act, a miscon-

59

ception of the character of God, has produced thousands, even millions, of unbelievers and skeptics. Many have been driven to insanity by the harrowing thought of unsaved loved ones writhing in the never-ending torments of hell. I am convinced that the popular teaching that there is a subterranean cavern where the wicked are tossed about on mountainous billows of liquid fire, and that such a place actually exists at this very time, this very minute, and is destined to continue without letup, age upon age, is a doctrine that has done untold harm to the Christian cause. Men and women are simply not able to reconcile the doctrine of eternal torment with the wonderful truth of God's undying love.

We read about Robert Ingersoll in a previous chapter, but let me say here that he might have become a prince of preachers instead of one of the foremost infidels, had it not been for his misunderstanding of this truth. His father told him when he was but a child that there were infants in hell not more than a span long, and that they were destined to burn throughout eternity. And Robert said, "If that is what God does, I hate Him." His logical mind could not conceive of such injustice; and, as a result that gifted intellect veered off into doubt and unbelief.

A friend of Ingersoll wrote him about what the Lord Jesus Christ had done for him personally, and asked, "Bob, how can you get up before an audience of intelligent people and run down a religion that will do this for a man?" That champion of unbelief read the letter to his audience one night, and then said, "Ladies and gentlemen, I am not running down a religion that will do that for a man. I am not preaching against a religion that will lift up downtrodden men, but I am preaching against a religion that some preachers preach."

But I ask you, Where in all the pages of Holy Scripture is the doctrine of eternal torment found? I have not been able to find it in my Bible. I do not believe you will find it in yours. I find there a hell—a literal, burning hell. But it is not the kind of hell that has been used to frighten men for centuries.

True, if there were at present a burning hell to which all sinners were consigned as soon as they die, then millions must be suffering torture there at this moment, for Jesus said, "Wide is the gate, and broad is the way, that leadeth to destruction, and many there be which go in thereat." Matthew 7:13, KJV.

But my Bible tells me that punishment will not be meted out until the end of the world. Jesus said, in explaining one of His parables, "As therefore the tares are gathered and burned in the fire; so shall it be in the end of this world." Matthew 13:40, KJV.

Evidently hell is not burning now. Evidently the lost are not being punished now. Evidently they are quietly waiting for the day of judgment. That's what the apostle Peter said: "The Lord knoweth how to deliver the godly out of temptations, and to reserve the unjust unto the day of judgment to be punished." 2 Peter 2:9, KJV.

Isn't that reasonable? Isn't that fair? How could it be otherwise?

Think it through. Would God send a man to hell before he has been judged? Would He let a man writhe in the fires of damnation for centuries and then in the day of judgment send someone to tap him on the shoulder and call him up to the bar of God to see whether he ought to be in hell or not? Can you not see what a libel upon the character of God such reasoning turns out to be? Is it not blasphemy of the character of God to suggest that the endless groans and shrieks of suffering creatures held in the flames of hell would be music to His ears?

I ask you, Could the justice of God ever be vindicated if He would consign Cain, the murderer of one man, to thousands of years more punishment than some modern murderer of thousands? For that is what it would be. If some madman, with the blood of thousands on his soul, were cast into hell today and burned for all eternity, he could never catch up with Cain. I ask you, Is that justice? Is that something that a God of love would do?

No. Yet these are just some of the problems and inconsistencies inherent in the traditional teaching of eternal torment. When we realize with what false colors Satan has painted the character of God, how he has sought to clothe the loving Creator with his own spirit of cruelty, is it any wonder that a God of love has been misunderstood, feared, and even hated?

God will punish sin. There is no question about that. Those who flatter themselves that God is too kind and merciful to administer justice have only to look at Calvary. They have only to look at the suffering Son of God, who bore sin for us, to know that "the wages of sin is death." And every soul who refuses the sacrifice made at such a cost must one day bear in his own person the penalty of his transgression.

God will punish sin. The power and authority of Heaven will be employed to put down rebellion. But the way it is done will be perfectly consistent with the fact that God is love.

But you say, "I am confused. I know that somewhere in the Bible I have read about everlasting fire." Let me describe this "everlasting" fire again. You may remember its explanation in the series on the book of Revelation in *Amazing Prophecies*. Repetition on such important matters is helpful.

Yes, you have. Suppose we read it again: "Then shall he say also unto them on the left hand, Depart from me, ye cursed, into everlasting fire, prepared for the devil and his angels." Matthew 25:41, KJV.

There it is. Everlasting fire. But now notice verse 46: "And these shall go away into *everlasting punishment*: but the righteous into life eternal."

It is the punish*ment*, you see, that is everlasting—not the punish*ing*.

Now what is the punishment of the unsaved? Paul says, "The wages of sin is death; but the gift of God is eternal life." Romans 6:23, KJV. Therefore we might read these words of Jesus this way: "These shall go away into *everlasting death*, but the righteous into life eternal." The punishment is death. And the death will be everlasting. The state of being dead will never end. Do you see?

Everlasting fire. Everlasting in its effect. But that does not mean that the fire will continue burning forever.

Follow me carefully. Did you know that in the book of Jude, verse 7, it says that the cities of Sodom and Gomorrah were destroyed by "eternal fire?" You remember what happened to those corrupt cities. But are they burning now? Of course not!

Another text that has caused perplexity in many minds is Revelation 20:10. It says, "And the devil that deceived them was cast into the lake of fire and brimstone, where the beast and the false prophet are, and shall be tormented day and night forever and ever." KJV.

Here we read that Satan, guiltiest of all, will "be tormented day and night forever and ever." Yet through the prophet Ezekiel, speaking to Satan and describing his future punishment, God says: "Therefore will I bring forth a fire from the midst of thee, it shall devour thee, and I will bring thee to ashes upon the earth. . . . And *never shalt thou be anymore.*" Ezekiel 28:18, 19, KJV.

An apparent contradiction, you see. But please know that God's Word never contradicts itself. Sometimes our preconceived ideas, our misunderstanding of its terms, may lead us to feel that it does. But the difficulty is in our own understanding. Just as we go to the dictionary for the meaning of English words, we must let the Bible explain its own terms.

For instance, in 1 Samuel 1:22 we read that Hannah promised Samuel to the Lord "forever." Yet verse 28 explains, "*As long as he liveth* he shall be lent to the Lord."

There you have it. As long as those condemned shall live, as long as consciousness lasts, they will be tormented. For some it may be only a few moments. For Satan it will be longest of all. You remember that Jesus said in one of His parables, "And that servant, which knew his lord's will, and prepared not himself, neither did according to his will, shall be beaten with many stripes. But he that knew not, and did commit things worthy of stripes, shall be beaten with few stripes." Luke 12:47, 48, KJV.

God does not delight in punishment. It is His strange act. But sin must be eradicated. In fairness to the universe there is no other way to deal with sin—with rebellion. This planet, if one sinner were left on it, would be a deadly virus forever threatening the universe. But I say again that the way rebellion is put down will be perfectly consistent with the character of a God of love.

The destruction of the lost will be quick. And it will be complete. Says Malachi, "The day cometh, that shall burn as an oven; and all the proud, yea, and all that do wickedly, shall be stubble: and the day that cometh shall burn them up, saith the Lord of hosts, that it shall leave them neither root nor branch." Malachi 4:1, KJV.

Stubble. A quick, hot fire. And remember, you do not put stubble into the fire to preserve it. It is quickly burned up.

Notice Psalm 37:20, 10, KJV: "But the wicked shall perish, and the enemies of the Lord shall be as the fat of lambs: they shall consume; into smoke shall they consume away." "For yet a little while, and the wicked shall not be: yea, thou shalt diligently consider his place, and it shall not be." The enemies of the Lord will be burned like fat. They will consume into smoke. They will cease to be. Even their place shall not be. Could words be clearer?

The destruction will be final. "They shall be as though they had not been." Obadiah 16, KJV.

The fire will be literal, and it will be unquenchable. No shield of neutrons will prevent the fire from falling. But when it has done its work, it will go out. The effects of the fire are eternal—but not the burning.

That is the Word of God. Does it sound like the superstition of the Middle Ages? Does it sound like devils with horns and tails and pitchforks tending the flames to keep them from going out?

No. You will find nothing of the kind in the Sacred Volume. From cover to cover you will find nothing but a God of justice, mercy, and love.

Do you not see how kind and merciful and just God's plan is—how much better than the way men have long misunderstood it? I have known men and women who were disappointed temporarily, until they thought it through, to learn that their loved ones who have died are not now in heaven. But I have never known a soul who was disappointed to learn that his unsaved loved ones are not now in hell. Never forget that the two go together. If the one is true, the other is true. But how often I have seen the relief and joy that have come to men and women as they have realized that their unsaved loved ones are not writhing in torment at all, but are quietly sleeping.

But someone says, "What about the rich man and Lazarus? Surely that parable contradicts what you are saying."

Remember, please, that it is a *parable*. For that is the key to understanding it. A parable is a story, true or fictional, told to teach a lesson or truth, and its details are not necessarily to be interpreted literally. It is not safe, therefore, to build upon the details of a parable a doctrinal concept that is taught nowhere else in Scripture. In a parable, for instance, life and action are sometimes attributed even to inanimate objects, for the sake of illustrating truth. In Judges 9:7-15 the trees are represented as talking together and anointing a king. Are we to accept this story as proof that trees can talk?

Read the story of the rich man and Lazarus, in Luke 16:19-31, and then ask yourself if Jesus meant the details of the story to be interpreted literally. Did He mean that all the saved are literally in the bosom of Abraham? Did He mean that heaven and hell are not only in sight of each other, but within speaking distance? Did He mean that the saved must be forced to watch the torments of the unsaved? Did He mean that heaven and hell are so close that a drop of water on the tip of the finger could be carried across into the flames? And would such a drop of water lessen the suffering?

No. Jesus was simply teaching that in the life to come the status of the rich man and the beggar would be reversed. Character, not wealth, will decide a man's destiny.

Where, then, did the whole idea of an eternally burning hell originate? It is a falsehood that was fanned into flame in the early centuries of the Christian era. It spread from paganism by way of Judaism into the Christian church, to be passed on to our unsuspecting generation as gospel fact. But it did not originate with the pagan philosophies of those early centuries. It dates back to those intentionally deceptive words of Satan in the Garden of Eden, *"Ye shall not surely die."*

"Ye shall not surely die"—you are immortal—you cannot die. That is the falsehood with which he trapped our first parents. And do you see where that reasoning leads? If you are immortal, if you cannot die, you must suffer eternally for your sins. That is where the whole idea of an ever-burning hell originated.

But God says, "The wages of sin is death"—not life, even in hell. Death is the penalty that man fears. Eternal death is the penalty he seeks to escape. He looks for a place to hide from it—no matter how uncomfortable that place may be. He wants anything but death. No wonder he has tried to find a refuge in the subtle suggestion, "Ye shall not surely die."

But that refuge will be swept away. The day will come when, in mercy to the universe, sin must be finally dealt with. The war for the control of the minds and souls of men must be brought to its finish. Satan has enthroned himself as the god of a rebel race. He must be dethroned and his character exposed before the universe for what it is.

God does not delight in punishment. The ultimate judgment upon sin and sinners will be His strange act. Nevertheless, that day will come. And when it does, it will be very, very real. The fire will be literal. It will be hot. And no device of man will be able to put it out.

The apostle Peter calls it "the day of the Lord." "But the day of the Lord will come as a thief in the night; in the which the heavens shall pass away with a great noise, and the elements shall melt with fervent heat." 2 Peter 3:10, KJV.

Follow carefully as we trace the events of that strange day.

"And the kings of the earth, and the great men, and the rich men, and the chief captains, and the mighty men, and every bondman, and every freeman, hid themselves in the dens and in the rocks of the mountains; and said to the mountains and rocks, Fall on us, and hide us from the face of him that sitteth on the throne, and from the wrath of the Lamb: for the day of his wrath is come; and who shall be able to stand?" Revelation 6:15-17, KJV.

Cosmic invasion! The Saviour of men descends the blazing skies. For some it will be the fulfillment of every hope. But for some it will not be a happy day. For in that day, position, power, prestige, possessions, will not cover. Strong men, weak men, unprepared men, will actually cry for the inanimate rocks to protect them—not from physical destruction, but from the searching eyes of one whom they have neglected or rejected. But from those loving eyes there will be no place to hide.

No place to hide. And "the wicked perish at the presence of God." Psalm 68:2. The very brightness of His appearing destroys them. Read 2 Thessalonians 2:8. And then, according to

Revelation 20:5, they "lived not again until the thousand years were finished."

The thousand years. Read the details in Revelation 20. (Revelation 20 was studied in a previous book in this set—*Amazing Prophecies*. But a review is needed here to picture the entire story.) Here is not a millennium of peace, as some have thought. And the lost, far from having a second chance during that time, simply sleep through it. But they live again at the end of the thousand years.

You see, there are two resurrections taught in Scripture. "Marvel not at this: for the hour is coming, in the which all that are in the graves shall hear his voice, and shall come forth; they that have done good, unto the resurrection of life; and they that have done evil, unto the resurrection of damnation." John 5:28, 29, KJV.

Two resurrections, you see. The resurrection of the saved—at the second coming of Christ—comes at the beginning of the thousand years. And the unsaved are resurrected at its close, for "the rest of the dead lived not again *until* the thousand years were finished."

Where are the saints, then, during this time? They have been caught up in the clouds at Christ's coming and have gone to "be with the Lord." The promise of Jesus has been fulfilled, "I will come again, and receive you unto myself; that where I am, there ye may be also."

Where are the lost? They sleep. And Satan, through this time, is confined to this empty world, bound by a chain of circumstances that he is powerless to break. For with all the saints in heaven, and every sinner dead, he has no one to tempt. He must wait in death row, condemned to die, for a thousand years. But "after that he must be loosed a little season." Revelation 20:3, KJV.

Shall we review?

At the beginning of the thousand years is the second coming of Christ. The wicked are slain by the brightness of His coming. The righteous dead are resurrected and, with the righteous living, taken to heaven.	In between, during the thousand years, all the righteous are in heaven, all the wicked are dead, and Satan is confined to this empty earth.	At the end of the thousand years is the second resurrection, the resurrection of the wicked. The wicked are finally destroyed, and the earth is purified by fire and made new.

But, you ask, "Why does not God finally destroy sinners at the second coming of Christ? Why does He wait a thousand years to do it, and then resurrect them only to destroy them?"

Simply this. God will not carry out His strange act until all the universe understands why He must do it—until you and I understand. There must not be a question in any mind in regard to His justice. That is why Paul speaks of a time when "the saints shall judge the world." 1 Corinthians 6:2, KJV.

The guilt of the lost has already been decided before Christ comes. But the saints become a kind of jury, which does not decide upon the guilt or innocence of men, but which vindicates the judgment of God. They become a jury, not because their help is needed, but because they need to understand God's dealings, need to know why men and women—some of them perhaps their own loved ones—are shut out of the kingdom.

And now, at last, the hour comes. No longer is there possibility of misunderstanding. No longer must God wait to make the universe clean. The city of God descends to this earth. The lost are called to life, now to meet their God.

Satan is loosed from his prison. And now, with sinners again under his influence, he instills in them his own hatred of God. The spirit of rebellion, like a mighty torrent, breaks forth again. He leads them over the desolate, war-ravaged earth in a last desperate attempt to take the City of God and establish himself as king of a rebel world.

But suddenly they stop in their tracks. Men and women stand in full view of the city that might have been their eternal home. With anguished hearts they look back upon their strange infatuation and cry out, "Take my money. Take my sinful pleasures. Take my procrastination and delay. These are what kept me from deciding for Jesus!" But it is too late. Their characters are fixed. A life of rebellion against God has unfitted them for the harmony of the earth made new. Its purity, peace, and praise would be torture to them. They would welcome death that they might be hidden from the face of the Saviour.

The whole world stands arraigned before the bar of God on the charge of high treason against His government. But the destiny of the lost is fixed by their own choice. Their exclusion from the joys of heaven is voluntary with themselves. And now they fall to their knees, acknowledging that God is just. "That at the name of Jesus every knee should bow; . . . and that every tongue should confess that Jesus Christ is Lord." Philippians 2:10, 11, KJV.

This is not true repentance. This is not real acceptance. Rebellion still would conquer if it could. They have played with eternity. But they do not now repent of their choice. They only regret its fearful result. Their confession now is the confession of Judas, "I have sinned in that I have betrayed the innocent blood."

No longer must God wait. Not a soul, now, will misunderstand His strange act. He calls out, "Let the fire fall!"

"And they went up on the breadth of the earth, and compassed the camp of the saints about, and the beloved city: and fire came down from God out of heaven, and devoured them." Revelation 20:9, KJV.

That is God's own description of hell. That is the only hell the Bible talks about. Remember the words of Peter? "The day of the Lord will come as a thief in the night; in the which the heavens shall pass away with a great noise, and the elements shall melt with fervent heat." 2 Peter 3:10, KJV.

And the prophet Nahum says, "The mountains quake at him,

and the hills melt, and the earth is burned at his presence, yea, the world, and all that dwell therein." Nahum 1:5, KJV.

Does it sound like atomic energy? Will God use atomic power to destroy rebellion on this planet? Does it sound like the power released by the fusion of hydrogen atoms? Does it sound like volcanoes—those molten mountains that blow their tops into the sky? History's spouting Krakatoas are burning evidence that there is fire stored up against that day.

Remember the first judgment—the Flood of Noah's day? Just as in that day waters from within the earth united with water from heaven to destroy the earth, so in the coming judgment fire from within the earth will unite with fire from heaven at God's command. The fire is there, awaiting His reluctant use. Study of the present formation of the earth indicates that a thousand and more Krakatoas, Mauna Loas, and Vesuviuses have been shaking and tearing at its foundation—most logically as the result of the Flood. The rocks bear evidence that these things have happened.

The thoughtful person, therefore, in contemplating world judgment through God's control of forces latent in the universe and stored within the earth, can begin to understand why the prophet compares the Flood of Noah's day to the day of judgment in ours. Listen!

"Whereby the world that then was, being overflowed with water, perished: but the heavens and the earth, which are now, by the same word are kept in store, reserved unto fire against the day of judgment." 2 Peter 3:6, 7, KJV.

That is the divine record. But intermingled in this statement of last things we read that the Lord "is longsuffering, . . . not willing that any should perish, but that all should come to repentance." Verse 9.

Said Ezekiel, "As I live, saith the Lord God, I have no pleasure in the death of the wicked; but that the wicked turn from his way and live: . . . for why will ye die?" Ezekiel 33:11, KJV.

What is God thinking as the flames envelop the earth? What is in His mind? Is it the exulting of a conqueror over an enemy bent before His power? No, it is the cry of a rejected Saviour, "Why will ye die?" It is the pathetic cry of a loving Father who called His children out of the burning and they would not come. "O Jerusalem, Jerusalem, . . . how often would I have gathered thy children together, even as a hen gathereth her chickens under her wings, and ye would not!" Matthew 23:37, KJV.

O New York, how often I have stood beside your spires of steel and called out over Times Square and Broadway. But ye would not hear!

O London, how often My voice has blended with that of Big Ben, tolling the lateness of the hour. But ye gave no heed.

O strange planet in rebellion, how long and patiently I have knocked at your towers of glass and urged you to let Me in. I would have saved you from the burning. But ye would not!

Do you begin now to understand God's dealing with sin? However terrifying, however literal, however final the fires of judgment, *remember what has gone before*. He who has called His children out of the burning and they would not come—it is He who finally calls out in bitter disappointment, "Let the fire fall!"

Such is the strange act forced upon infinite love by man's free choice! For those who have rejected His grace there will be no place to hide. But is that all? Smoke ascending from a doomed planet, never to return? And nothing more?

No. The City of God, with every soul who has made the Saviour his hiding place, will defy the flames, as the ark once defied the waters, while God destroys the last trace of sin from this planet and leaves it clean, beautiful, and new. Man's final destination, if he chooses, is not death, but life!

Who will be able to stand in that day? The answer is found in Psalm 91: "He that dwelleth in the secret place of the most High shall abide under the shadow of the Almighty." "He shall cover thee with his feathers, and under his wings shalt thou trust." "A thousand shall fall at thy side, and ten thousand at thy right hand; but it shall not come nigh thee. Only with thine eyes shalt thou behold and see the reward of the wicked." KJV.

That is true protection. Your God and mine desires above all else that you receive it.

The Telltale Connection

On the eighteenth of December, 1912, it was announced to the world that the remains of an early human fossil had been found in a shallow gravel pit near the village of Piltdown in the County of Sussex, England. Britain was proud, for the Piltdown Man was believed to be the earliest known human fossil.

But some forty years later another announcement was made. It had all been an out-and-out fake, the work of a person or persons unknown. Its lower jaw was not human at all, but that of a young female orangutan. Its teeth had been filed, and the hinge had been broken to prevent the discovery that it did not belong with the skull. British science was red faced.

Charles Dawson, the discoverer, became the prime suspect. And though he had died thirty-seven years earlier, a monument to him was promptly removed. Through the years a number of others were suggested as possible suspects, but Dawson was still the front-runner.

But there was someone else who had haunted the Piltdown site during the excavation. He was a retired medical doctor who knew human anatomy well. He was a chemist, much interested in both geology and archaeology, and an avid collector of fossils. More than that, he loved a good hoax. He loved adventure. He was a writer gifted in manipulating the most complex plots. And a motive was not hard to find, for he bore a grudge against the British science establishment. Who was He? None other than the creator of Sherlock Holmes: Sir Arthur Conan Doyle!

73

So it was that John Hathaway Winslow, a writer of our own time, found himself on the trail of the greatest fictional detective of all time—Sherlock Holmes, whose exploits became required reading for the police forces of several nations. Winslow went public with his astounding findings in the September issue of *Science 83*. And I think you'll agree that the case against Sir Arthur, though circumstantial, is convincing to the point of being overwhelming.

Sir Arthur lived only seven or eight miles from the excavation site, and it appears that he visited it openly in 1912. Here was a doctor no longer in practice. At this stage, he was enjoying the rewards of a successful author. He was a prodigious walker, who often set forth on long jaunts. There is little doubt that he often visited the relatively unguarded site, or passed next to it and peered over the hedge to observe progress. All he had to do was watch out for the excavators.

The most difficult task was to concoct a convincing creature, stain it to match the color of the Piltdown gravel, and surround it with appropriate fossil remains and implements. All this he was more than competent to accomplish.

How could he have obtained the jawbone of an orangutan? A former neighbor of his had recently returned from the Malay Peninsula, where his brother was head of the Malay museums. And one of his museums had just purchased a large collection of animal specimens from Borneo. Orangutans live only in Borneo and Sumatra.

How would Sir Arthur know how to file teeth to make them simulate human wear? Early in his medical practice he had moved into a house previously occupied by a dentist. Heaped about in great numbers were casts of human jaws.

How did he get just the right skull? He had a friend who had an immense collection of skulls and often sold them to those interested.

Some of the fossil mammal remains planted by the hoaxer were later identified as coming from the Mediterranean. How could Sir Arthur have obtained them? He and his second wife had recently honeymooned on the Mediterranean and had visited the most likely sites. The timing of his travels was perfect.

On and on the clues fit together like pieces of a puzzle. But what about a motive? Why did he hold a grudge against the science establishment? Here, too, the evidence is convincing.

Arthur Conan Doyle was not only fascinated with science, but in his later years he had become a firm believer in Spiritualism. On the other hand, scientist Edwin Ray Lankester was a dedicated Darwinian evolutionist, probably evolution's staunchest defender. And he had no use for Spiritualists. He held them up to ridicule and was merciless in his attacks. He believed their claims were fraudulent, and he wanted desperately to catch them in the act.

For that purpose, he attended a séance in the company of the American medium Henry Slade, who was the rage of British Spiritualists in the mid-1870s. There was to be communication with a spirit, and the spirit would write a message on a slate. But just after the slate was shown to those present, to demonstrate that it was clean, and before there was any noise of writing, Lankester grabbed the slate and discovered a message already on it. A magistrate agreed that fraud had taken place. And Henry Slade left England as quietly and quickly as possible.

Sir Arthur was very unhappy about this exposure, and complained that it was not right to condemn all Spiritualists because of one instance of fraud. Sir Arthur and Lankester were not friends!

Would it be surprising at all if Arthur Conan Doyle, master-creator of fiction that he was, should find exquisite delight in bringing the same sort of embarrassment to British science that Lankester had brought to the Spiritualists? What more natural motive could there be?

Yes, *the telltale connection* that links Arthur Conan Doyle to Piltdown Man is very, very strong!

But there are other links, other ties, other connections that we must explore. Some interesting. And some very significant, linking even the two opposites, so often antagonistic to each other—evolution and spiritism. The one calling itself science; the other considered antiscientific.

In the days of Arthur Conan Doyle the theory of evolution

had already done more than anything else to destroy faith in the Bible and in God Himself. But this left men and women adrift on a sea of chance—without a future, without hope. So where did they turn? By the thousands they turned to the psychic world, to the séance, to psychic phenomena—in an effort to replace what they had lost.

But there is a stronger tie between spiritism and evolution. For both reach back to the early morning of this planet. We find there the beginning of spiritism and its promises. And we find there the record of the first use of a psychic phenomenon to attract an audience.

True, we find no theory of evolution in the book of Genesis. But we do find, in the very first verse of the Bible, the clear statement that God is the Creator. It reads like this: "In the beginning God created the heaven and the earth." Genesis 1:1, KJV.

And it is that simple statement which evolution refuses to believe. Its challenge of God's creatorship and its substitution of a man-made theory of our beginnings in its place—here is the heart of evolutionary teaching.

Have you ever noticed that the quarrel of unbelievers with the Bible is usually concerned with the early chapters of Genesis? Evolution ties back to that book as an open challenge of God's credibility.

In the case of spiritism, we find its beginning in the story of man's fall, recorded in the third chapter of the Bible. And there God is openly charged with not telling the truth.

Now I know that the story of man's fall is widely considered just a bit of folklore, amusing folklore at that. Give someone the clue, "She ate the apple." And you will get the response, "Eve." And the fact that there is no mention of an apple in the Genesis story is an indication of how little attention has been given to what happened there.

I ask you, *Could it be that Genesis 3 is not folklore at all, but rather the first boom of cosmic cannons in a continuing and escalating war that explains every strange thing that is happening today?* Let's look at this all-too-familiar narrative—this time in language we will all understand.

Imagine, if you will, the impossible. Imagine that you were a cosmic reporter assigned to cover the creation of the planet Earth, to be an actual eyewitness to it all.

It was an exciting week, accompanying the Creator and His entourage of angels as He moved down through the star-studded corridors of space—with galaxies and flashing suns on every side, and angel harps tuned their highest.

Then you reached a lonely spot near the edge of God's universe. You saw Him step out into the emptiness and speak words filled with all the power of the Infinite. The thunder of His voice resonated to distant worlds. And suddenly there it was, where a moment before there was nothing: a planet fresh from the Creator's hand, spinning in perfect orbit!

The whole week was spectacular beyond words. You've used all your best adjectives—and failed even to approach the reality. And then, on Friday afternoon, came God's masterpiece of creation, made in His own image—Adam and Eve!

You were glad when you were permitted to stay on, to cover further developments. But that prospect was not completely bright, for you knew that all was not well in God's universe. Heaven's highest and most privileged angel, one named Lucifer, had become dissatisfied over nothing. It seems that his own beauty convinced him that he ought to have the place of God. He was especially angry over the fact that the Son of God was to be the One to actually speak the planet Earth into existence. Why not Lucifer?

He had to be banished from heaven. There was no other way. But now he is here. And you remember how furious he was when he saw the exquisite beauty of the planet God had fitted up for Adam and Eve. You heard him cursing God and plotting to make this earth the headquarters of his rebellion.

The problem is that God has created Adam and Eve with the power to choose. He doesn't want any of His subjects to be robots. So this happy pair *could* rebel. It *could* happen. And that would be tragedy for the human race!

You heard God talking to Adam. And He said something like this: "Adam, I have given you the power to choose. You are not a robot. I will set before you life and death. And I expect you to be responsible for the choice you make. I hope you will choose life. But the decision is yours."

And God said to Adam, "I want to give you never-ending life. That is my plan. But I dare not give you immortality until I know you can be trusted with a life that never ends. In order to test your loyalty I have placed off bounds one tree in the Garden—just one tree. If you eat of its fruit you will be separating yourself from the Source of life, and you will die. That isn't a threat, Adam. Death is just the natural result of rebellion. I hope you will act responsibly. But you must choose. I cannot choose for you."

You were listening, too, the day God told the happy pair about Lucifer. He told them that He would not permit the fallen angel to follow them around the Garden. He could tempt them only if they approached the one forbidden tree. Adam and Eve talked it all over. And they couldn't imagine such a terrible thing as rebelling against the Creator they loved.

Then came that fateful day. Eve was walking alone as she approached that tree. Walking alone—and wondering aloud why God had placed that one tree off bounds. It didn't look dangerous. It was as beautiful as all the other trees. The serpent was sitting on one of its branches, contentedly eating the fruit. And the serpent began to talk to Eve. And she knew that serpents didn't have the power of speech, even in the Garden of Eden. She didn't know, though she should have known, that she was witnessing the first psychic phenomenon in this earth's history, that here was a daylight séance, with the serpent acting as a medium for the fallen angel.

You watched as the serpent invited the woman to eat, assuring her that it couldn't harm her. After all, wasn't he eating it himself?

You weren't the only one who wanted to cry out to warn her. Angels were watching. God was watching. But no one must interfere. You watched in breathless horror as she reached out, took the fruit, and ate. And then, when she felt no harm, she filled her arms with the beautiful fruit and took it to her husband.

You'll never forget the look of shock and terror in Adam's

face when he saw what Eve had done. He knew that she must die. And he couldn't bear the thought of losing her. He didn't stop to think that God could create another companion for him—one as lovely as she. He just rashly, deliberately, knowing the consequences of his act, determined that if Eve must die, he would die with her. And the whole human race had, at that moment, entered the age of tears!

Well, you weren't there. And I wasn't there. There was no press coverage. There were no television cameras. No press conferences. It wasn't that the press was barred. There wasn't any press!

Let's read it—just as the Bible tells it. First, this is what God told Adam. This is the warning, given in the deepest love and concern: "The Lord God commanded the man, saying, Of every tree of the garden thou mayest freely eat: But of the tree of the knowledge of good and evil, thou shalt not eat of it: for in the day that thou eatest thereof thou shalt surely die." Genesis 1:16, 17, KJV.

Was this a threat? No. Is it a threat if I tell you that if you jump from the top of the Empire State Building you will die? Of course not. God was only telling Adam what the consequence of a wrong choice would be.

But the serpent openly contradicts what God has said. Listen: "The serpent said unto the woman, Ye shall not surely die: For God doth know that in the day ye eat thereof, then your eyes shall be opened, and ye shall be as gods, knowing good and evil." Genesis 3:4, 5, KJV.

The battle is out in the open. The fallen angel has charged God with being untruthful, with withholding the highest good from His subjects. He's still making the same charge today. And millions are believing it!

Think about *this* for a moment. If the fall of man was not planned or programmed by the Creator, it follows that *it didn't have to happen*. Let us suppose, then, that Adam's wife, rather than entering into conversation with the serpent, had turned pale at the sight and sound of a serpent talking, and had set the world's first track record in her flight back to the safety of her husband's company.

If only the story of Genesis 3 could be rewritten!

Or what about *this*? God is all-powerful. Nothing is too hard for Him. That conversation between Eve and the serpent took only a few short moments. Adam's decision took only seconds. Time is under the control of its Creator. Why couldn't He just lift that short segment of time out of history and close it up as if it had never happened? Should the destiny of the human race depend upon the decisions of a single hour?

But no! A God of love and integrity would never stoop to such manipulation of events. He will never deceive His subjects about what has gone before. The tragic story of man's fall cannot be deleted. It cannot be rewritten. It happened just as the book of Genesis tells it. The woman saw a serpent talking. She listened. She believed. And *belief was the enemy!*

Do you realize what a strong link there is between deception and death? Seldom does one deceive another for any good purpose. Certainly not the fallen angel. He deceives men and women with only one thing in mind—to utterly destroy them. When he peddles his deceptions, he is peddling death—death from which there is no recovery, no resurrection. And you'll be amazed to see the variety and the attractiveness of the packaging he uses!

Yet in spite of the endless variation, the constant changing of labels, and the ever more alluring giftwrap, the strategy of the fallen angel and his invisible army of angels-turned-demons is still the same today as it was in the Garden of Eden. His use of disguise. His use of a medium. His use of psychic phenomena to capture a mind and throw it off guard. His challenge of God's integrity. His suggestion that God is withholding that which is good. His promise that you will never die, no matter how you live. His promise that rebellion will lead to a state like that of the gods. These are the earmarks of the great deceiver's philosophy.

Remember his words, "Ye shall not surely die." And "ye shall be as gods." Watch for them. For no matter where you find them, and no matter how cleverly they are rephrased, they shout one warning, "Lucifer was here!"

Yes, you will be shocked to your toes as you see what is going on in the unseen world!

This generation, unfortunately, is an easy mark for anything sensational, anything supernatural, any package that comes complete with miracles. Ours is a generation that loves magic. It is fascinated by the unknown, by the invisible, by auras and pyramid power and biorhythms and whatever is new.

Millions are saying, "Entertain us. Excite us. Show us magic. Dazzle our eyes with the supernatural. Boggle our minds. Mystify us. Cast a spell over us. Overwhelm our senses. Sweep us off our feet. Promise us fun and fame and heaven too. And we'll follow you anywhere!"

The generation honored with the personal presence of Jesus was not unlike our own. Constantly, it was demanding, "Show us a sign that You are who You claim to be. Light up the sky at midnight. Leap off the pinnacle of the temple. Strike the hated Romans dead. Give us a sign!"

But Jesus never confused magic with power. He came not to manipulate minds, but to transform them at the sinner's request. He came not to take the throne, but to be crucified. Not to be a King, but a Sacrifice. He said to those who demanded to know His identity, "When you have lifted up the Son of Man, then you will know who I am." John 8:28, NIV.

"When you have lifted Me up. When you have crucified Me. When you have scorned and mocked and laughed at Me. When you have driven spikes into My hands. When you have hung Me between heaven and earth on a despised Roman cross and dared Me to come down if I could. When you have left Me to die without even a drink of cold water. *Then* you will know who I am!"

And yes, when He hung there on that splintery cross, they knew. The thief on the cross beside Him knew who He was. The Roman centurion knew. And the enemies of Jesus knew. The haughty Caiaphas. And Pilate. And many a man left that cross with tortured conscience and unclean hands because he had joined with the mob in crucifying the very Son of God!

That generation, and ours, had been given a sign—the sign of the Son of God dying in man's place. There is no greater sign!

You and I will have to decide whether we want a magician or a Saviour. And there's no better time than now to make our choice!

Playing Games With Death

The legend says that it happened in the streets of Baghdad.

A merchant sent his servant to the market. But soon the servant returned, trembling and greatly agitated, and said to his master, "Down in the marketplace I was jostled by a woman in the crowd, and when I turned around I saw it was Death that jostled me. She looked at me and made a threatening gesture. Master, please lend me your horse, for I must hasten away to avoid her. I will ride to Samarra and there I will hide, and Death will not find me."

The merchant lent him his horse, and the servant galloped away in a cloud of dust.

A little later the merchant himself went to the marketplace and saw Death standing in the crowd. He said to her, "Why did you frighten my servant this morning? Why did you make a threatening gesture?"

"That was not a threatening gesture," said Death. "It was only a start of surprise. I was astonished to see him in Baghdad, for *I have an appointment with him tonight in Samarra!*"

Only a legend—out of the streets of Baghdad. But it paints a graphic picture of the fatalism that is gripping countless minds today. For millions of frustrated individuals have decided that this weary planet, with every man on it, has an appointment with the death angel—its wings bathed in atomic power and propelling us swiftly to oblivion.

We try to forget. We spend long hours in the pursuit of pleasure and profit. We fall in love with toyland. We protest what is happening. We rebel against a future that we cannot control. But sooner or later, even in the busy marketplace, man is jostled by the death angel, rudely reminded of her presence. And what else can he do but begin a wild ride to Samarra, hoping to find someplace to hide, some barrier behind which death shall forget to look?

Death is on the way out. Because of what Jesus did on Calvary, death will one day be destroyed. But in the meantime, death is still on the loose. And this planet is the cemetery of the universe—the place where everyone dies!

A little child in Northern Ireland saw his father gunned down at his own front door. Night after night, following that tragedy, little David would scream as he relived that terrible moment in his dreams. Night after night he would kneel by his bed and say, "Please, God, can't Daddy come down from heaven just for a minute so I can see him? I won't keep him. I'll let him go back."

Why didn't God answer that little boy's prayer? Is there a reason? Doesn't God care?

Yes, of course He cares! And yes, I believe there is a reason.

I believe, too, that the cruel enemy of us all, who loves nothing better than to deceive and destroy, would gladly take advantage of little David's tears and *appear* to answer his prayer. Hundreds of times, in a cloak of false compassion, the fallen angel has *seemingly* brought back a loved one, just for a minute, so he could be seen and even touched.

There is lying and fraud and trickery in the psychic world. But there is no mistake more dangerous than to believe that it is *all* fraud and trickery. Jesus warned us concerning our day, "For false Christs and false prophets will appear and perform great signs and miracles to deceive even the elect—if that were possible." Matthew 24:24, NIV.

No one is in greater danger than the man who thinks spiritism is all magic and trickery and fraud, just waiting to be exposed by someone as discerning as himself. Because someday something will happen to *him*—something that can't be explained away. And he'll tumble right into the trap!

Ever since it first coldly introduced itself on this planet, death has been a mystery. Everybody dies. So it is only natural that we should want to know what happens on the other side of this final experience. But in our day the popular interest in death is approaching an obsession. There are classes in death and dying, manuals on how to die. Mothers rock their dead babies, and fathers hammer in the coffin nails. Dying is treated as an adventure, a romance.

But I am uncomfortable about all this cozying up with death. What if it becomes not only an obsession but an involvement, a cozying up with the fallen angel who is the author of death?

This generation, like those before it, continues to play its dangerous games with death. But in our day something new has been added. For now we are bombarded with the stories of those who say they have personally experienced death and have come back to tell us about it.

You've heard the reports—all strangely similar. Leaving their bodies. Long, dark tunnels. Then grassy slopes. And a being of light. And they don't want to come back to their bodies. Most significant of all, these people aren't afraid of death anymore. And they don't believe the Bible anymore. They think they have found a better source of information.

Were these people really dead? Or just *near* death? Evidently they were not irreversibly dead, for all were resuscitated. Evidently these experiences are just the malfunctioning of a mind almost gone. There are many similar out-of-body experiences in drug literature.

But if these stories represent simply the misfiring of a mind near death, how is it that hundreds of minds are misfiring in almost the same way? Something is going on here. Something strange. Is it possible that some external power, some intelligent and highly motivated entity, may be stepping in to control these weakened and malfunctioning minds? If so, who would be suspect? Who could be so motivated?

Some say these experiences prove that there is life after death. But do they—if those involved didn't really die? And some say these reports prove that the Bible is true. But how can they be supportive of the Bible when they are in strong disagreement with it?

How are they in disagreement? In what they say about what happens at death. Listen to this clear scripture: "The living know that they shall die: but the dead know not any thing." Ecclesiastes 9:5, KJV.

The verse that follows is also interesting, for it says: "Also their love, and their hatred, and their envy, is now perished." Ecclesiastes 9:6, KJV.

There is an equally strong statement in the Psalms. "Put not your trust in princes, nor in the son of man, in whom there is no help. His breath goeth forth, he returned to his earth; in that very day his thoughts perish." Psalm 146:3, 4, KJV.

According to the Bible, the dead know nothing. Their thoughts have perished. Certainly there can be no communication with those who don't know anything and can't think. The Bible has the dead quietly sleeping in their graves till the day of the resurrection when Jesus calls them to life. They know nothing of what is happening to loved ones who still live. According to the Bible we do not go to our reward at death, one at a time. Rather, our Lord has planned that we all go together when He returns. The resurrection is the hope of the Christian. Listen to the words of the apostle Paul as he describes it: "The Lord himself shall descend from heaven with a shout, with the voice of the archangel, and with the trump of God: and the dead in Christ shall rise first: Then we which are alive and remain shall be caught up together with them in the clouds, to meet the Lord in the air: and so shall we ever be with the Lord." 1 Thessalonians 4:16, 17, KJV.

What a day of reunion! Friends and loved ones long separated by death—now together again, nevermore to part. Little children carried from their graves by angels and placed in their mothers' arms. What a day! Would you want it any other way? Would you want to settle for some grassy slope?

Did you notice that, according to these recent reports, everybody goes to the same reward, the same grassy slope—regardless of how they have lived? It is that way in all of spiritism. Good and bad alike all go to the same place. There is no judgment to determine what a man's reward should be.

And did you notice that no one sees God or Jesus on those

grassy slopes? But there is a being of light. And it is reported that that being of light even laughs at their sins. Would Jesus ever laugh at sin—when it was our sins that crushed out His life?

Can you guess who that being of light might be? Listen to this: "And no marvel; for Satan himself is transformed into an angel of light." 2 Corinthians 11:14, KJV.

Do you see whose philosophy it is that runs like a thread through all of this? Do you see *the telltale connection?* Do you see how it all ties back to the words of the serpent in the Garden of Eden? "You will not surely die." That's what the fallen angel said then. He's still saying it in a thousand ways. Only now he's calling it science. And thousands who would never go near a séance are swept into the net!

These experiences haven't proved a thing—except that Satan, just as the Bible says, is furious because he knows that his time is short. Spiritism is sweeping the world. And only those who know the Bible, and hold onto it for dear life, will escape!

"You will not surely die." The whole house of spiritism would collapse overnight if that false concept were not so readily accepted by fallen humanity. But voices everywhere are echoing those words. And millions are believing the lie!

It's only one more step to the epidemic of seeking altered states of consciousness that is rampant today. And long with this, fitting like a glove, is the idea of a universal energy that flows through man, making him the possessor of divine power, making him a part of God. Remember? "You will be as gods."

And if man, simply by connecting himself with this psychic force, tapping this universal energy, can make himself a god, what need has he of a Saviour? What need has he of repentance? Guilt can be forgotten—now that the power of God is within himself!

Do you see how dangerous these ideas are—and how fatal?

But that is just what Satan wants. He knows that he himself is doomed. And he has determined to take the whole human race with him to destruction—if he can!

That's why he is telling this generation that death is not so bad after all, that it is nothing to fear, that no one ever really dies. That's why he tells everyone who will listen that there is no judgment, that good and bad all go to the same place, regardless of how they have lived. He is bribing men and women with a false hope that God calls a "refuge of lies."

But that refuge of lies will be swept away. No man can escape death by cozying up to it and calling it a friend!

Listen! Are you satisfied to look forward to nothing but a little bit of grass, approached by a long, dark tunnel? Are you interested at all in a future that has no place for God and Jesus? What sort of paradise would it be if all the mass murderers and rapists and madmen were there to terrorize eternity?

Wouldn't you rather have the heaven that Jesus has prepared for you—where sin and death and heartache and tears are forever shut out? A place that is lighted by the glory that streams from the throne of God. A place where there is no night. A city with gates and streets and fabulous homes that are real—with your name over the door of one of them. Where you can see Jesus face to face. Where yours can be the companionship of angels. And friends and loved ones will never part again!

And there's so much more! Flowers that never fade. Leaves that never fall. Beauty beyond description. Space travel to other worlds. Endless opportunities to explore and understand God's vast creation. Nothing will be left out that could possibly contribute to your happiness!

This is the heaven that Lucifer lost. This is the home that will never be his again. That's why he's determined that you shall never experience it. He's going to belittle it—play it down—ridicule it—counterfeit it—lie about it. And he'll smile in hellish glee if you decide it's nothing you want! But the choice is yours. You don't have to miss out!

Today the way seems long and weary. It may seem that the long night of tears and trouble will never be finished. But it will, friend. It will. Swiftly, so swiftly, it will change. Think what it will be to breathe the freshness of the morning and know that it will never end. Suddenly it's heaven! Suddenly it's home!

Think about that home. Think about it often. Let it fill your mind. Let it give you something to live for. Let it take your loneliness away. The Saviour wants you to have it. Even now He is out on the road calling your name. Calling you to Himself. Why not take His hand just now—and let Him lead you home?

Psychic Counterfeits

Dark clouds scowled over Lhasa, the mysterious forbidden city of Tibet. The year was 1855. And the Dalai Lama was dead!

It was believed that a Mongolian hermit had slipped poison into the ruler's butter tea. But the hermit had escaped. And *someone* must be punished!

Late that night, in the temple room of the Potala—the thousand-room palace of the Dalai Lama—a séance was called. The Oracle, the state prophet of Tibet, would invoke the gods to learn who had killed their supreme lama.

Tempu Gergan, the wealthy and respected minister of finance, stood nervously at the edge of the group. He had been warned that afternoon that he might be named the culprit. And he knew it was not unlikely, for only recently he had accused the Oracle of being unreliable. Would he pass by an opportunity for revenge?

All was now ready. The Oracle sat on his throne, wearing the ceremonial robes. On his head was a massive helmet of silver and gold, embellished with five human skulls.

A high lama wafted incense into the seer's face. Behind him a choir of priests chanted weirdly. Facing the Oracle, a living Buddha in a spine-chilling chant was calling upon the three-headed, six-armed demon-god to take possession of the seer.

"Come hither, mighty Pehar. Tell us who killed the Dalai Lama."

Tempu's breath was choking him. He wanted to scream. But a hypnotic spell kept his eyes on the Oracle.

91

The face of the Oracle had undergone a terrifying change. It was no longer the face of a priest, but the leering face of Pehar. The Oracle was now fully demon-possessed!

Tempu stood cold but perspiring. The ground seemed to sway beneath him as he watched from behind a pillar.

"I see a golden cup with a demon dancing upon the brim," muttered the Oracle. "There is a strange priest offering the cup to the Dalai Lama. He wears a high-peaked hat and tattered garments."

He was describing the Mongolian. But the demon voice went on, "I see around the holy one bags of gold and silver. A hand offers the silver to the strange priest. The face—I cannot see the face. Yes, it is coming—"

Tempu knew instinctively that he would be named. He flung himself out the door and down the passageway. Pausing only a moment in a small room, he discarded his rich brocades and strode on as a peasant pilgrim. But already he could hear a crescendo of voices, "Tempu Gergan is the man! Seize him!"

He wanted to dash madly away. But he must look like a poor pilgrim. Would the eternal stairs never end?

Finally he was clear of the building and headed for the city wall. He heard a shout behind him, "Block the stairs! No one must leave the palace!"

He had escaped just in time. Silently he slipped over the wall where a trusted servant waited with two horses.

He had escaped. But he would never see his beloved city of Lhasa again. An innocent man would spend the rest of his days in exile—all because of an unreliable priest, aided by lying demons!

You say, "I would never attend a séance or have anything to do with demons. So I'm safe."

But don't be too sure!

The winds are blowing out of the East with gale force. Western fascination with Eastern mysticism can no longer be considered a passing fad. True, the traditions of Eastern worship are filtered through Western secularism to make them appear less threatening. But they are here—and here to stay. Basic occult philosophy—fresh-labeled and unrecognized—is pervading our society. Transcendental meditation has been taught in our schools—as science. It has become popular to talk of past lives—and karma. And, believe it or not, it is said that firewalking—yes, walking across hot coals with bare feet—could be called almost a trend in southern California.

But call it what you will, Eastern worship is built upon a concept completely foreign to the gospel of Jesus Christ. Eastern religion, like nearly all false religion, is a gospel of salvation by works. It is man saving himself.

Call it what you will, Eastern meditation is not science. It is a religion. Regardless of claims to the contrary, it is Vedantic Hinduism. Its initiation rite is a religious ceremony. Its mantras are related to Hindu deities. And its goal is to attain the state of Hindu God-realization, to recognize our true self as divine.

Call it what you will, reincarnation, with its karma, is a cruel counterfeit of the cross of Calvary. It is man saying to God, "I don't need a Saviour. I'll pay for my own sins—even if it takes a thousand lives to do it!"

Don't you hear in it all the echo of the serpent's words, "Ye shall not surely die" and "Ye shall be as gods"? The telltale connection is too plain to miss!

And call it what you will, Eastern mysticism is riddled with demons. Listen to this: "They made Him jealous with strange gods; with abominations they provoked Him to anger. They sacrificed to demons who were not God, to gods whom they have not known, new gods who came lately, whom your fathers did not dread." Deuteronomy 32:16, 17, NASB.

Have you ever wondered how it is that people, century after century, can bow down to gods of wood or stone—gods that cannot think—hideous gods that no worshiper could love—gods that they would escape if only they could? Have you blamed it to the backwardness of the East?

No, it isn't all backwardness. The power of those Eastern gods is not in the wood or in the stone. It is not in the idols themselves. It isn't their hideousness alone that inspires fear. It's the demons that inhabit them. Listen to what the apostle

Paul says: "What do I mean then? That a thing sacrificed to idols is anything, or that an idol is anything? No; but I say that the things which the Gentiles sacrifice, they sacrifice to demons, and not to God; and I do not want you to become sharers in demons." 1 Corinthians 10:19, 20, NASB.

Can we reach into the Eastern fire and not be burned? Can we take to ourselves what looks harmless—and close our eyes to the Satanism, the human sacrifice, the demon possession, and all the rest?

There seems to be a death wish at work in Eastern mysticism. There are demon gods that stand at the gate of death and beckon the worshipers through. Like the serpent in Eden, they make death the door to the future—and the door to becoming a god. What a cruel hoax!

But has the fallen angel exhausted all his resources in the East? No. Never. He isn't limited to a little black bag or a tool box. He has a whole supermarket of subtle, unrecognized, mislabeled, gift-wrapped offerings just waiting for unsuspecting customers who think they are safe because they've never attended a séance!

Yes, you have to be wide awake and on your toes to keep from bumping into some slender thread of the web he is building around this whole planet!

Ever since the fallen angel began stalking the human race in the Garden of Eden he has been engaged in a desperate race for the minds of men. And he hasn't left a single avenue to the mind unexplored or unexploited!

Rock and roll. Harmless, you say. Just too loud. That's why you ask your teenagers to shut the door. But Bob Larson, former rock-and-roll performer and composer and now national radio commentator, has a different opinion. He says, "Rock and roll is the agency which Satan is using to possess this generation en masse. I have seen with my own eyes teenagers who have become demon-possessed while dancing to rock and roll music."

He points out that "there is no difference between the repetitive movements of witch doctors and tribal dancers and the dances of American teenagers." Both have the same hypnotic beat and the same potential for demon possession.

And listen to this—also from Bob Larson, author of *Rock and Roll, the Devil's Diversion.* Read especially pages 133-136.

"One of the most uncanny stories I have ever heard was related to me by a close friend of mine. For several weeks he dealt with a sixteen-year-old boy who by his own admission communed with demon spirits. One day [the boy] asked my friend to turn on the radio to a rock and roll station. As they listened, this teenager would relate, just prior to the time the singer on the recording would sing them, the words to songs he had never heard before. When asked how he could do this the sixteen-year-old replied that the same demon spirits that he was acquainted with had inspired the songs. Also he explained that while on acid trips he could hear demons sing some of the very songs he would later hear recorded by psychedelic rock groups."

What do you think of that?

Yes, the fallen angel is peddling his wares everywhere—under a thousand false labels. And if they were all exposed for what they really are, he would have a thousand more. But keep in mind that he would not be so successful if he were not offering what this generation wants!

For instance, this generation doesn't want the responsibility that goes with belief in a Creator. It prefers to trace its origin to some ancient sea or to some cosmic accident. Or to Von Daniken's astronauts. Von Daniken, the author of three well-known books, may not know how to reason logically or consistently, but he knows how to jimmy the facts to fit his changing and contradictory theories. And he knows how to sell books!

The truth is that today's liberal society is open to *any* alternate to the Genesis account of creation.

And millions today prefer to get their guidance from the stars rather than order their lives by the only safe guide—the Word of God. This in spite of the complete unreliability of the horoscopes they follow.

A French statistician by the name of Michel Gauquelin has been putting astrology to the test for more than twenty years, reports the June issue of *Science 84.* On one occasion he put out a newspaper ad offering free personalized horoscopes. A hundred and fifty people responded. To each of them he sent the same identical horoscope and asked how well it fit. Ninety-four percent said they recognized themselves.

It was the horoscope of mass murderer Dr. Marcel Petiot!

Well, doesn't our Lord have something better for us than that? I believe He does. This is what He says: "I will instruct thee and teach thee in the way which thou shalt go: I will guide thee with mine eye." Psalm 32:8, KJV.

What could be better than that? To have our Lord personally guide us. Not the stars, but He who made the stars!

But now listen to what He says through the prophet Isaiah. We'll read it from the Today's English Version:

> "Let your astrologers come forward and save you—
>   those people who study the stars,
>   who map out the zones of the heavens
>   and tell you from month to month
>   what is going to happen to you.
> They will be like bits of straw,
>   and a fire will burn them up!
> They will not even be able to save themselves."
>   —Isaiah 47:13, 14.

Our Lord doesn't want us to be deceived. He doesn't want us to be conned by the enemy. He doesn't want us to get off the track and lose out in the end. That's why He expressly forbids His people to have anything to do with the occult—not just the astrologers, but the whole occult system. Listen to this: "There shall not be found among you any one that maketh his son or his daughter to pass through the fire, or that useth divination [fortune-teller], or an observer of times [astrologer], or an enchanter [magician], or a witch, or a charmer [hypnotist], or a consulter with familiar spirits [medium possessed with a spirit or a "guide"], or a wizard [clairvoyant or psychic], or a necromancer [medium who consults the dead]. For all that do these things are an abomination unto the Lord." Deuteronomy 18:10-12, KJV.

And I think you know what abomination means! Evidently

our Lord just isn't on very good terms with the occult. He just doesn't want His people to be deceived and drawn into the devil's net!

Yet the very things God has forbidden are increasing in popularity every day! Yes, we have an enemy who is determined to destroy everyone he can. He would destroy the whole human race right now if God would permit it. He delights in violence and war. He loves to see masses of people swept into sudden death without a chance to repent.

To bring about this destruction he will use every disguise he can, every deception he can, every lie he can. He is delighted when men and women think he doesn't exist, or when they think of him as a horrible monster with hoofs and horns. Such ideas leave them completely unprepared for meeting him as an angel of light.

The fallen angel's hatred of God, and especially of Jesus, knows no bounds. He is determined to counterfeit everything that is true and right and good. You have seen how he has counterfeited the future life, how he has distorted the facts about death. You have seen how he takes advantage of loneliness and tears and offers the false comfort of communication with the dead.

Satan is the great impersonator. And he has millions of helpers, invisible to us, who are almost as clever as he in impersonation. Remember that they are all fallen angels, with the intelligence of angels and with supernatural power. And they have had thousands of years of experience in their work of deception. They watch us, know all about us, and then trap us—too many of us. They impersonate dead people—and living people. They pose as residents of other worlds. They will yet try to counterfeit the second coming of our Lord. And Satan himself will impersonate Jesus. And almost everybody will bow down!

Do you begin to see what is going on in the invisible world? Our only safety is in letting the Lord Jesus lead us through this treacherous end time that is so mined with deception!

"Beneath the cross of Jesus
        I fain would take my stand,
The shadow of a mighty rock
        Within a weary land;
A home within the wilderness.
        A rest upon the way,
From the burning of the noontide heat,
        And the burden of the day."

The Truth About Psychic Healing

I have here two newspaper articles. This one, dated January 11, 1978, and clipped from the *San Francisco Chronicle*, is titled "Skeptics of Mind Power Call It Superstition." And it says:

"If you suspect that UFOs may be real. . . . If you think the Bermuda Triangle is a dangerous place. . . . If you lend even half an ear to any of these beliefs—and there seem to be millions of Americans who do—well, man, there are some scientists and scholars who are mighty worried about you.

"They think you are being gulled, and they see the rise of cult and occult as a sickness of our times. For them the issue is science versus superstition."

But only a little more than six years later, on April 3, 1984, the *Oakland Tribune*, just across the bay from San Francisco, carried an extensive article entitled "Psychics get foothold in the sciences." It carries over onto much of page two and is followed the next day by a second part. It is favorable in tone and could be summed up in these few words: "If psi works, why not use it?"

Are we about to witness a wedding of psi and science? It just could be. Did you know that John F. Kennedy University in Orinda, just beyond the Oakland hills, actually has an accredited parapsychology department?

Parapsychology has wanted all along to be known as a science, and for that reason has kept very quiet about its ties with the occult. Yet its strongest evidence comes from mediums, and without mediums it would collapse.

Parapsychology is the study of occult phenomena. And you can't go very far in the study of occult phenomena without encountering psychic healing in some form. Most every spirit medium has some ability to heal. You see, then, that the various forms of psychic healing are actually a subdivision of parapsychology.

Now science and psi, science and the occult, Western medicine and psychic healing, have wanted nothing to do with each other. But things are changing, in spite of the fact that parapsychology still calls itself a science. More and more physicians are endorsing psychic, or mediumistic, healing. And the door is being opened slightly even to witchcraft.

Physicians make up a large part of the 1,500-member Academy of Parapsychology and Medicine, which gives much of its attention to research and psychic healing. Its president, Dr. Robert A. Bradley, is a medium. He is the inventor of the Bradley method of natural childbirth, which, he says, is an idea he received from one of his spirit guides. The primary purpose of the academy is to integrate science and medicine with the occult.

In Great Britain, the World Federation of Healers, with 9,000 members, has been given government permission to treat patients in 1,500 hospitals in that country. And this same federation, made up largely of professed mediums, has been given membership in the United Nations Association.

Former astronaut Edgar Mitchell, a parapsychology enthusiast, is said to be working hard to integrate psychic healing with traditional medicine. He believes that "psychic healers can become valuable adjuncts to hospital staffs, to general practitioners and to clinics." Yet there is something strange about his enthusiasm, for he also says that the power of psychic methodology "can be as dangerous as atomic energy; in reality I think it is even more so."

Strange, isn't it, to be so enthusiastic about something that dangerous?

Some qualified medical doctors are actually referring patients to mediums and occultists these days—to men like Dr. Robert Leichtman, for instance, who is a physician, psychic, and psychic researcher. He diagnoses from the spirit world. But word of his abilities has spread fast among his fellow MDs, and he diagnoses several hundred cases a year for them, with accuracy above the 90 percent level.

Dr. Elisabeth Kübler-Ross, the famous authority on death and dying, is deeply involved in the occult, along with her partner and friend Dr. Raymond Moody, author of best-seller *Life After Life*. It is said that Kübler-Ross has five spirit guides. "Salem" is her favorite.

Yes, things are changing. Science and psi are putting away their differences. And hypnosis is now everyday stuff.

"But wait!" you say. "What's wrong with hypnosis? It doesn't have any connection with the occult, does it?"

Well, you decide.

You've heard of mesmerism and its animal magnetism, popular in the last century. The mesmeric trance and the spiritistic trance were one and the same. And every occult phenomena found in mesmerism is found in modern hypnosis. Both are spiritistic, though Anton Mesmer, like the parapsychologists of today, preferred to identify with science. In essence, modern hypnotism *is* mesmerism.

In Satan's race for the minds of men, for the control of the will and the conscience, it is only natural that hypnotism should be one of his favorite tools. For he knows that hypnosis is a direct avenue to the mind. And he knows that when the mind is surrendered to another, even for some seemingly good purpose, he or one of his helpers can step in and take control. The gate is open.

Never forget that the conscience operates through the mind. When the mind is abdicated, so is the conscience. And never forget the fact that the mind once breached, the lock once pried, is never so strong again!

And the trouble is that reading labels doesn't help much. For hypnosis may even be slipped in under so harmless-sounding a label as "scientific relaxation."

Ever hear of Silva Mind Control? Or the new defunct Mind Dynamics? Classes like these promise you almost everything.

And testimonials are glowing. One girl insisted, "Besides

finding that you can have anything you want, that you are the reason for everything, you also find that you can't be sad or depressed anymore." Is it any wonder that people sign up?

But Dr. Elmer Green, an outspoken critic who has even debated one of the groups on television, points out that most of these companies use nothing more than variations of hypnosis. He says that students in these organizations "go through a four-day program of intense hypnotic education in order to do the things they demonstrate."

Do you see now why Solomon, the wise man, gives us this counsel? "Keep thy heart [your mind] with all diligence; for out of it are the issues of life." Proverbs 4:23, KJV.

Well, what about yoga? You say, "I do yoga exercises. But that's just a way to relax the body and the mind. It's not Hinduism at all. And no demons are involved. So it's perfectly safe."

Are you sure?

The goal of yoga, says researcher John Weldon, is "for the yoga devotee to realize that he is one with Brahman, the highest impersonal Hindu God." And the physical exercises are designed to prepare one to receive this idea into his mind and body. Yoga is pure occultism. And meditation is the operative principle of yoga.

There are tremendous risks in the practice of yoga, especially Kundalini yoga. For a single mistake can mean insanity or sudden death. And demonic power is never far away.

Jesus spent a great deal of His time in healing. He spent more time in healing than in preaching. His compassion for human suffering knew no bounds. He didn't want anyone to hurt.

Wouldn't you expect, then, that the enemy—the fallen angel who is out to destroy all he can—wouldn't you expect him to give a high priority to counterfeit healing? And believe me, he hasn't missed the chance!

Psychic healing is becoming more popular every day. Nobody wants to die. And when life is threatened, men and women will go anywhere, and pay any price, for even a promise of being well again.

There are psychic diagnosticians who follow in the steps of Edgar Cayce, who first developed his diagnosis from hypnosis.

Some healers achieve an accuracy approaching that of Cayce. Some of them never see the patient. Some of them use a device, such as a rod or pendulum, in their diagnosing. But the power is not in the device. It is in the operator. And the degree of success is proportionate to the degree of the healer's involvement with the spirit world, with the occult. Most of them know that spirits do the healing. But not all wish to identify themselves with the demonic. They may say the healing comes from their own "higher self."

Did you know that Cayce came to be much concerned about the nature of the power that operated through him? The time came when he suspected that "the devil might be tempting me to do his work by operating through me when I was conceited enough to think God had given me special power."

But Cayce, like so many others, was trapped. He was unable to outsmart or to stop the forces that worked through him.

There is something very interesting about psychic prescriptions. Some of them are just simple, harmless, old-fashioned ideas. And some of them are for the latest drugs—even though the healer may have no medical training whatever and may not even be able to read. He may be simply repeating what a voice in his ear is telling him.

And think about this: Some of these psychic prescriptions may not work at all if used by a physician with no occult ties. And some of them may be dangerous if used by a non-psychic physician, but perfectly harmless if used by an occult healer. In one instance a potent drug was prescribed in a quantity that would kill a dozen people, but evidently the healer's patient was unharmed!

Keep in mind that often a psychic diagnosis is wrong. Time is lost and real harm done. And even when apparent healing does take place, it is usually temporary. Often the illness is simply transferred to another part of the body—or worse, to the mind!

But whatever may be said to the contrary, there are cures. The supernatural is at work. And there are some undeniable miracles of healing. If you are ill—even terminally ill—there are places where you can go and be healed. But are you willing to pay the price? And do you know what the price is?

A patient appeared at the door of a healer who had been making some striking claims in newspaper ads. She told the healer that the doctors had diagnosed her as having a serious blood disease, possibly leukemia.

The healer replied, "I'm not a medical doctor. I treat with the mind and use hypnosis. The medical profession doesn't have a cure for leukemia. But we have cured leukemia. We have cured cancer, even terminal cancer." Then she outlined the procedure that she would use.

"Lend me your mind," she said, "to remove the debris and get your mind functioning properly." The mind would then purify the blood, and the body would then function as it should.

The patient turned out to be a policewoman who had secretly recorded the conversation. The healer was later arrested.

Notice. "Lend me your mind." I say again, There are places where you can go and be healed. But the price of healing is the surrender of your mind. Are you willing to pay such a staggering price? Are you willing to sell yourself into lifetime slavery to the spirit world, to the enemy of the Lord Jesus?

Some, of course, even with their eyes wide open, are willing to make such a fearful bargain. Listen to this from the psychic surgeon Edivaldo: "If the devil can relieve pain, open up a stomach and remove an ulcer, then I prefer the devil!"

We come now to psychic surgery. I confess that not many months ago I believed that all psychic surgery was outright fraud, accomplished by sleight of hand. But I know better now. Much of it *is* fraud, perhaps the majority of it. But not all of it. Some of it is frighteningly supernatural.

The majority of the psychic surgeons come from the spiritist centers of Brazil and the Philippines. One of the best known is the late Arigo, who attended from three to four hundred people a day—a total of more than two million before his fatal accident.

Psychic surgery is done under unsanitary, even filthy conditions, often with dirty or rusty knives as instruments. No anesthesia is used. And the surgeon pays little attention to his work. Obviously this is because a spirit guide, or spirit doctor, is really performing the surgery. The surgeons are all aware of this and freely admit that they can do nothing without the spirits.

Spirit surgery, along with spirit diagnosis and spirit healing, is coming into our own country. Is this the healing you want? Are you willing to pay the price of a slavery to the occult from which only the Lord Jesus Christ can ever free you?

We hear much about holistic medicine today. And certainly the concept of treating the whole man, of a patient's involvement in his own health care, of preventive medicine—this is all good. Jesus treated the whole man. And for many years before anyone heard of holistic medicine the motto and goal of Loma Linda University's medical school at Loma Linda, California, has been "To Make Man Whole." Seventh-day Adventists have long been promoting this concept.

But with the holistic medicine that is being marketed today there is need of caution. There is need of discernment. We must be able to distinguish between that which is safe and that which is not safe. For some of the trappings of psychic healing have already filtered deeply into holistic medicine. And some things that in themselves are good are now in bad company.

How great is the influence of Eastern mysticism and the occult in the holistic health movement? It is overwhelming. It appears that the movement as a whole is dominated, if not controlled, by philosophies completely incompatible with Christianity. Nearly all of the holistic techniques are filled with subtle, and not so subtle, implications that have their origin in the occult. Most of these techniques are designed to produce altered states of consciousness to make their treatments work. And the new energies of the East—dangerous in the extreme!

It is apparent that few of the holistic centers around the country have escaped occult involvement. Their literature reveals this. The courses they teach give it away. It is estimated that probably 80 to 90 percent of the talks given at national holistic health conferences support the occult in one way or another.

You can see, then, that the role of the individual physician to whom we entrust our health care becomes vitally important.

Certainly it would be unfair to assume that an individual physician is involved with the occult just because many of his colleagues are. On the other hand, the time has come for extreme caution. It is no longer safe to assume noninvolvement!

You may be saying, "All this is very interesting. Amazing. Even frightening. I've learned a lot."

But friend, until you realize that evil angels are all about us in the unseen world and that they are battling for the control of our minds—yours and mine—you've missed the point. These agents of Satan, if permitted, will distract our minds, disorder and torment our bodies, and destroy our health, our possessions, and our lives. And they will try to use everything that happens to us—everything good and everything bad—to accomplish our total destruction!

On the other hand, Jesus will do *everything He can* to save us. He is stronger than the enemy. And He would sooner send every angel from heaven to our aid than let us pass under the enemy's power against our will!

But we must *ask* for that aid. It will not be forced upon us. You and I, this very moment, with our own permission, are under the control of one power or the other. But the choice is ours!

Wonderful Jesus! What we have learned about the enemy only makes us love Jesus more. For the beauty of His character, in contrast, stands out like a brilliant star against a black night!

Are you letting every enemy attack drive you nearer to the Saviour and deepen your relationship with Him? I hope so. For only in His hands are any of us safe!

Toys of a
Fallen Angel

What are those mysterious lights that cavort like cosmic dancers across the night sky? Flitting across the radar screens of the mind—only to disappear. Following us. Eluding us. Dazzling us with their technology. Luring us with their mystery. Baffling us with their uncanny tricks.

What are these strange things that bob up and down like illuminated yo-yos over our hilltops and our highways, our airports, and our cities—defying our restricted air space, skittering away when we point a powerful beam of light their way, and generally frightening us out of our wits?

Are they the toys of some cosmic prankster? Or could it be that *people*—people like you and me—are the toys? Toys of a fallen angel. To be played with a little while—and then thrown away?

It is said that the Rand Corporation, the fabled "think-tank," was once asked to feed UFO data into a computer and fight an imaginary war with the elusive entities. But since we didn't know their origin or their technology or how to attack their bases, the computer advised that we surrender!

Am I going to tell you the UFOs are real? No. Am I going to tell you they aren't? No. It doesn't matter whether they are real or not. Something very real is happening to millions of people. And that *does* matter!

Let me say it once more. Whether or not UFOs exist is not the question. Whether they do or not, something is going on. People are involved with something—whether it is real or unreal. People are letting their lives be completely changed by UFOs. People are making a religion out of UFOs. People are blowing their minds, and losing their minds, over UFOs. People are being injured by UFOs. People are being controlled by UFOs. We need to stop quibbling over whether they are seeing them or not or riding in them or not or telling the truth about them or not—and get on with the business of discovering, if we can, the source of the phenomena. For that we desperately need to know!

It isn't being gullible to recognize that something is going on. The man who is gullible is the man who closes his eyes and his ears and refuses to admit that anything is happening. He is the one being fooled. We have come to a time when it isn't safe to stick your head in the sand—if you care anything about your head!

Something is going on. And nothing is gained by trying to tell experienced pilots that the planet Venus is roaming around between them and the ground. Nothing is accomplished by telling a pilot that the squadron of brilliantly lighted craft that executed incredibly difficult maneuvers at high speed, frighteningly close to his plane, was nothing more than plastic garment bags, with lighted candles inside, released by some teenage boys. Whenever debunking becomes ridiculous, it only acts as a boomerang that quickly destroys the credibility of the debunker!

In our American democracy it seems that we have only two options. We can be a Democrat or be a Republican. And it's like that with UFOs. It is *assumed* that we have but two choices. These strange craft are all nonsense. Or they are extraterrestrial. One or the other.

But I don't believe that we are limited to only two possible explanations. My Bible tells me about a host of intelligent entities, *terrestrially* based, who could easily be back of the whole phenomenon. Listen to what it says: "There was war in heaven. Michael [Christ] and his angels fought against the dragon [Satan], and the dragon and his angels fought back. But he was not strong enough, and they lost their place in heaven. The great dragon was hurled down—that ancient serpent called the devil or Satan, who leads the whole world astray. He was hurled to the earth, and his angels with him." Revelation 12:7-9, NIV.

Verse 3 suggests that a third of all the angels of heaven sided with Satan in this senseless rebellion and were banished to the earth with him. That's a lot of angels—angels now turned demons.

Now, I don't want to be dogmatic and say that Satan is the source of the UFO phenomenon. Again, I don't know what UFOs are. They might turn out to be some secret military craft. Some remotely controlled spycraft. Or ball lightning. Or something we haven't thought of yet. But certainly there is a mountain of evidence that points to Satan and his demon helpers as prime suspects.

Here we have a vast number of intelligences once extraterrestrial, created to inhabit heaven, but now operating right here on this earth. And they have the advantage of being able to work invisibly, hidden from our sight. And though banished to our planet, they still have the brilliant minds of angels. They know more about technology than men have ever dreamed. And they have supernatural power, within the limits that God has set.

Jesus warned us that in this end time our planet would be overrun with false prophets and false miracles. He said, "False Christs and false prophets will appear and perform great signs and miracles to deceive even the elect—if that were possible." Matthew 24:24, NIV.

Did you notice? Miracles to deceive. That's why the miracles are worked.

And now to the book of Revelation. "They are spirits of demons performing miraculous signs." Revelation 13:13, 14, KJV.

It's speaking of an agent of Satan here. And notice. It doesn't say "miracles which he tried to do" or "miracles which he pretended to do." It says "miracles which he had *power* to do." And those miracles are for the purpose of deceiving those who dwell on the earth.

It's a good thing to get these things straight, don't you think, before we go on.

I think you will agree that the fallen angel, with his army of demon helpers, is well equipped to engineer a phenomenon such as we are discussing. There is no part of it, no feature of it, that is beyond his power.

But I want to say again, It really doesn't matter whether UFOs exist or not, whether they are real or only an illusion. If they do exist, it doesn't matter whether they are made of metal or made of hallucinations. We only mark ourselves as having faulty eyesight if we say nothing is happening. Whatever they are or are not, millions of people are involved with them and are being harmed. They are making a religion of them. And whether Satan is originating the phenomenon or not, he is certainly exploiting the situation to the full!

I know that many attempts have been made to explain the sightings as due to natural causes. For years they have been blamed to the moon, to temperature inversions, light refractions, migrating birds, clouds, mirages, stars, marsh gas, ball lightning—and of course the planet Venus.

But there are patterns in the sightings that soon rule out such explanations and indicate that intelligence of some kind is back of the UFO activity. For instance, in a great many cases the UFOs fly right up to a state line but do not cross it. Why don't they cross it? Certainly meteors cannot read our maps. There are more sightings in isolated areas and in the late evening, suggesting that UFOs, or their occupants, usually prefer to keep their activity secret. There are more sightings on Wednesday and Saturday nights. Can the phenomenon read not only our maps, but also our calendars and our clocks? Some intelligence must be involved. And it doesn't take long to see that the phenomenon is not natural but supernatural.

It is also sensational. And I am aware that some people think we ought not to talk about anything sensational. But that's what Satan and his helpers love. Ever since the encounter in the Garden of Eden it has been their favorite and most successful area of attack. And to refuse to mention anything sensational is to say to Satan, "Look! You just stay within the boundaries of the sensational and we won't bother you."

And that gives the fallen angel and his helpers a free hand!

So. Let's talk about it. Ever hear of poltergeists? Of course. Noisy ghosts. Did you know that almost always when there is a flap of UFO sightings there is also a flap of poltergeist activity—just before or just after or simultaneously? There's a connection somewhere.

To study the endless sightings of UFOs is not very productive. There are books full of them—and books full of messages that have supposedly come from them. But they are repetitive, and they are boring. It is far better to study the people who see these things—the people who have contact with them. It's the people who are important.

These millions of people from all walks of life, including a great many pilots and policemen—these people are not lying. They may be the victims of lies. But they are describing as truthfully as they can what they saw and what happened and what they have been told!

Strange things happen to people who see these baffling things in the sky—especially to people who have any further contact with them. Their lives soon become a series of bizarre experiences, and anything—or any combination of things— may happen. Their telephones and television sets go berserk. Radios play when they are turned off. Fierce headaches, nausea, and loss of appetite are common.

They are troubled by nightmares. They see frightening apparitions. Poltergeists invade the homes. They have strange visitors and strange phone calls. Mysterious black Cadillacs may appear and disappear suddenly. And the more frightened they become, the more the manifestations escalate!

Soon after the first contact the personality may begin to deteriorate. And the deterioration may become total. Paranoid-schizophrenia and even suicide may result.

This does not for a moment mean that a person who sees a UFO is insane. Not at all. But unless the involvement is broken off, he or she may be *driven* insane by the phenomena.

Did you know that the symptoms experienced by UFO contactees are the same as those of demon possession? Dabbling with UFOs can be extremely dangerous. Even serious investigators take great risks. The conflict between Christ and

Satan is not folklore. It is real. Demons are real. And demons are treacherous.

We are dealing here with intelligences who are able to alter the perceptions and produce paranormal states of consciousness. They are able to alter the observer's sense of reality. Powerful imagery is projected upon the mind for the purpose of altering the individual's beliefs and making him a tool of the system of deception.

This may explain the reports of contactees being abducted and taken aboard a UFO. It seems that hypnosis can trigger the account of an abduction experience in almost anybody—that is, anybody uninformed enough and unwise enough to submit the mind to somebody else. This may explain why the abduction stories are so similar—just as the near-death stories of tunnels and grassy slopes and beings of light are similar. We are dealing here not simply with hypnosis, but with thought implant. The subject remembers what the entity in control of his mind wants remembered.

It is probable that these contactees were never taken aboard a flying saucer at all. Remember that these entities are able to manipulate the mind and induce a trance state. If you were to come upon a contactee at the time of his alleged kidnap experience, you might find him standing rigid beside his car or alongside the road. He is not going anywhere at all. What is happening to him is happening only in his mind. It has been implanted there.

Do you begin to see now how dangerous any involvement with UFOs can be? Take the "kidnap" experience, for instance. You may say, "If it never happened, how can it be dangerous?" But nothing is more dangerous than what happens to the mind. The individual *thinks* the abduction happened. And his whole life may be changed by that distortion of reality. And of course that is what the phenomenon is all about. Its goal is to alter belief and behavior and make the contactee a tool of the system.

Well, are the mysterious flying machines really up there in the skies? They are when the demons want them to be!

The UFOs go where they please and when they please. They go merrily on their way, baffling us with their inconsistent behavior, exasperating us with their elusive maneuvers, driving us crazy with their cruel games. And the wise man is he who knows, or at least suspects, who they are—and leaves them alone!

Perhaps we are ready now for the question, Do UFOs really exist at all? Evidently they do not exist in the way a book or a house or a plane exists. But certainly the *phenomenon* exists.

John Keel's book *UFOs Operation Trojan Horse* is probably the most informative and logical book written on the subject. After four years of investigating UFOs—full time, often day and night and without a vacation—he concluded that there are two general types of unidentified flying objects. They might be called the "soft" craft and the "hard" craft.

The "soft" objects are those that are luminous, that change shape and color at will, that split apart, that appear and disappear before your eyes, baffling explanation. These are the more numerous. And these are evidently the real phenomena. They can only be explained as manifestations of demon power. No other explanation makes sense or fits the facts.

Witnesses, over and over again, have confided in hushed tones to John Keel, "You know, I don't think that thing I saw was mechanical at all. I got the distinct impression that it was *alive!*"

Then, in much smaller number, there are the hard, seemingly solid objects that are seen occasionally. These have been fired upon by bullets—and the bullets have ricocheted off. They sometimes leave prints on the ground when they land. In flight, they frequently drop pieces of metal. John Keel believes that these seemingly hard, metallic UFOs are temporary manipulations of matter and energy, made for a few moments of use—or perhaps a few hours—probably to try to prove that they are real, or just to confuse.

In other words, they are materializations such as are seen in spiritism, where frequently there are materializations of ashtrays, bookends, trumpets, etc. And the "ufonauts" dematerialize the craft at will. That's the disappearing act.

The parallels between spiritism and the UFO phenomenon, between demonic activity and UFO activity, are striking. Mediums go into a trance. Contactees go into a trance. Spirits walk through closed doors. UFO entities seem to fly up to their ships and walk or float right through the sides. In both fields human beings and nonhuman objects are transported without visible means. Entities in both fields are able to change their shape at will. Both demons and UFO entities are able to assume the form of human beings—and frequently do.

Devotees of spiritism receive messages supposedly from deceased loved ones. UFO followers receive telephone calls supposedly from space people. Followers of both receive messages that are mentally detected—they hear them in their heads. Both see monsters and apparitions. Hypnotism ranges freely through both fields. Hoaxes are common in both. Demons are accomplished liars. So are UFO entities. Mediums are possessed and controlled and manipulated. So are contactees. Both become not only reporters but mouthpieces.

Do you see *the telltale connection*? Is there any question but that the same powers who operate in the darkened room may also be piloting their cosmic toys?

The man who becomes involved with UFOs in any way is in great danger. But the man who denies the existence of the phenomenon may be in even greater peril—because he is unprepared for the personal encounter that may be in store for him. To deny the reality of the unseen world is to be engulfed by it!

What do these elusive entities want? What is the purpose of all this worldwide propaganda? What is all this leading up to? You will see. And I promise you it's something bigger than you think. What we are witnessing is not overkill. This army of deceivers is not preparing to swat a fly. They have a real extravaganza in mind!

Satan and his demons would love nothing better than to destroy us all—now. But lacking God's permission to wipe out the human race, they will content themselves with making toys of the uninformed and the reckless. Be assured that Satan has no love even for his own. He toys with them a little while, plays mischievous games with them, feeds them nonsense, laughs at their troubles, and then throws them away like paper dolls that have begun to tear!

But friend, not one of us are toys to Jesus. Each one of us, to Him, is of infinite worth. The value of one soul can never be estimated except as we see what it cost Him to set it free!

See Him walking straight on, with His eyes on Calvary—never turning aside, never turning back. Because you were lost. And the only way to save you was to die in your place. See Him in face-to-face combat with the enemy, gaining for you the victory that could never be yours without Him!

See Him in Gethsemane, tempted to the very limit of His endurance. So tempted that He would have died right there in the garden had not an angel come to sustain Him. See Him struggling through His fearful ordeal while His closest friends are sleeping. See Him on the cross, with only the prayer of a thief to cheer Him. He heard no other prayer that day—except His own!

Why didn't He come down from the cross and call a legion of angels to lift Him out of the cruel nightmare of this Golgotha? Why didn't He give up—when it seemed that nobody wanted to be saved anyway? But no. Somewhere a few would accept His sacrifice. And even if only one—He was willing to die if only just one could be rescued from this doomed planet. That's how much He cared—and still cares—for you!

Whoever you are, wherever you are, whatever you have done, however great your guilt may be, He wants to forgive. He wants to be your Saviour. He wants to be your Friend. Your relationship with Him can be as close, as real, as enduring as if you were the only one in the world in need of His love and care!

To Jesus you will never be a toy. To Him you will always be a priceless treasure. He will never tire of you and throw you away. He will be your Friend forever. And you can be His!

The Tiger
Behind the Door

It was December 15, 1967.

Watching Lyndon Johnson turn on the lights of the Christmas tree was not exactly an exciting experience. Many of those who watched on television may have reacted with a measure of ho-hum. But not those who had heard the prediction!

Nineteen sixty-seven had been a big year for predictions. One after another, the prophecies had come down through mediums and psychics, astrologers and automatic writers, crystal-ball gazers and UFO contactees. Some of the predictions had failed. But others had come true on the nose—enough to make those in-the-know mighty nervous. All agreed that something big—and something disastrous—would happen when Lyndon Johnson pushed the switch. Possibly a nationwide power failure!

And so, glued to their television screens, they watched breathlessly. When the lights of the Christmas tree went on, would the lights of the nation go out?

The president pushed the switch. The lights of the tree went on. And nothing happened. But thirty seconds later an announcer's voice came over the noise of the crowd. "We interrupt this program for a special bulletin. A bridge with rush-hour traffic has just collapsed at Gallipolis, Ohio. Further details as soon as they are available."

The bridge at Gallipolis, Ohio. That could only be the 700-foot Silver Bridge that connected Gallipolis with Point Pleasant, West Virginia.

And Point Pleasant, for exactly thirteen months, had been

the target of some very strange goings-on. More than a hundred people had been frightened by a huge monster with red glowing eyes. It was shaped like a man, maybe seven feet tall, with huge folded wings. They called him Mothman. You can read about this in John Keel's book, *The Mothman Prophecies*.

But that was not all. People had been seeing UFOs all summer. There were dozens of witnesses.

There were the strange men in black, men who seemed unacquainted with the area, or even with this planet. Men whose shoe soles were perfectly clean after walking through mud, men whose features were strangely alike, men who wore thin clothing in the dead of winter. Men who talked like phonograph records speeded up.

There was Indrid Cold—he said that was his name. He said he was from the planet Lanulos. He drove a black Volkswagen—and sometimes a spaceship—and was generous with his strange and irrelevant information.

There were the black Cadillacs that kept disappearing when they were chased. With license numbers that no computer could trace. There were the strange phone calls, the phantom photographers, the TV sets that went berserk. For some Point Pleasant residents, everything seemed to be going berserk.

But neither Mothman nor Indrid Cold—nor any of the UFO entities, ever said a word about the coming disaster.

And then it happened!

Some who had seen Mothman—or been participants in other bizarre experiences during the year—went down with the bridge. Others would be claimed by death within a short time. Some would divorce. Some would suffer breakdowns and undergo long periods of hospitalization. A few would commit suicide.

Twelve UFOs were over Point Pleasant at the time the bridge went down. And some strange-looking men, wearing thin shoes in the cold, had been seen climbing on the bridge two days earlier. Was there any connection?

But if the strange entities knew about the coming disaster, or even participated in it, why hadn't they warned Point Pleasant?

We could ask the same question about Jonestown. With all the predictions from the various psychics, how is it that we were not warned that the horrifying suicide/massacre would take place?

I believe the answer to that question would not be difficult when we understand a little more about these psychic predictions.

I wonder if you are aware that six different psychics predicted the capture of Patty Hearst with uncanny accuracy. And the deaths of the Kennedy brothers and Martin Luther King were predicted again and again in different parts of the world.

Significantly, predictions like these, whoever the prophet and wherever the forecast is made, seem to be coming from a common source. Evidently there is a prediction syndicate operating somewhere!

The very same predictions are often fed through a number of different psychic channels. They are released through mediums and mystics, psychics and astrologers, automatic writers and crystal-ball gazers, Ouija boards and UFO contactees. Clearly they are all tuned in to the same source. UFO entities and spirit entities are part of the same gigantic system. The link is undeniable. In fact, the communication that takes place between a medium and the spirit world, the communication that takes place in the near-death experiences, the communication between UFO contactees and UFO entities, the communication between psychic healers and their spirit-doctors—in all these communicators on the other side, in the unseen world, are the same evil spirits, the same fallen angels, the same demons. They are simply adapting what they say to their particular audience.

Psychic predictions are often phrased identically, regardless of the channels through which they are released. This is true throughout the country—and throughout the world. The messages are often even *phrased* in the same way—no matter what language is used!

We can only conclude that psychic predictions have a common source. And if that source is ultimately Satan himself, it is not especially hard to understand why disasters like the Silver

Bridge—and Jonestown—were not predicted. For Satan genuinely loves disasters. And the more lives that are snuffed out, the more pleased he is.

Predictions in the year 1967 included a big power failure, New York sliding into the sea, the assassination of Pope Paul, plane crashes, a bigger power failure nationwide in scope, a disaster on the Ohio River, the Prime Minister of Australia disappearing, and explosions in Moscow.

All these happened on the nose, except the nationwide power failure, the assassination of Pope Paul, and Manhattan sliding into the sea. No location on the Ohio River had been pinpointed, so it was only a very general prediction. And the date on which the disaster happened had been linked by the entities—probably intentionally—with a nationwide power failure.

Do you see the pattern here? Some predictions come true. Some don't. In general, the minor ones are the most often accurate. The really major ones—like Manhattan slipping into the sea—are less likely to be accurate. Why is this?

Do these psychic entities know the future? Or don't they? Why isn't this giant prediction syndicate right all the time, if it knows the future?

The answer is that the entities do *not* know the future. Only God knows the future. And when He reveals it through His prophets, they are right all the time, not just some of the time.

The entities who run the prophecy syndicate do not know the future. But they know their own plans. They certainly do have an agenda for the future which they intend to follow if they can!

Keep in mind that God does restrict them to some extent and allows them to go only so far. But within the limits set by God, they are able to engineer many a disaster. It's a simple matter to arrange the collapsing of an aging bridge. They can crash planes—if God doesn't prevent them. They are often right about marriages and divorces, because they are able to listen in on the most private of conversations. They are present in the carefully-locked rooms where crimes are planned. And minds under the control of demons can often be influenced to carry out assassinations.

But pushing Manhattan or California into the sea is too

much for the fallen angel and his helpers. Nothing of such major consequence will happen unless and until God permits it!

Do you see now why the predictions of the psychics are usually concerned with marriages, divorces, plane crashes, assassinations, etc? The fallen angel predicts what he thinks he may
have a good chance of accomplishing. But the stately march of
prophecy that you find in the Bible—affecting nations and the
world, and penetrating the future with an accuracy that never
fails—is simply beyond these impostors!

But wait. Sometimes they do predict big things like the end
of the world, don't they? Yes, they do.

For instance, take the case of Dr. Charles A. Laughead. He
was a physician on the staff of Michigan State University when
he started communicating with entities who claimed to be from
outer space in 1954. A number of minor prophecies were passed
along to him, and they came true on the nose. Then came the
big one. The world was going to be split in two, and the Atlantic
Coast would sink into the sea. France, England, and Russia
would have the same fate. But a few select people would be rescued by spaceships.

Dr. Laughead and his friends were so impressed by the accuracy of the previous predictions that they took this one very
seriously. He made sober declarations to the press. Then on December 21, they gathered in a garden to wait for rescue. They
had been told not to wear any metal. So they discarded belt
buckles and clasps, pens and lighters, even shoes with metal
eyelets.

Then they waited!

It has happened again and again. Men and women become
involved. They are convinced by the accuracy of a few predictions. The entities smother them with promises—and then lead
them down the road to ruin. Jobs are gone, careers sacrificed,
families broken, health destroyed. They hide themselves away
and stare at the walls. And the embarrassment and shame and
frustration all too often lead to suicide or madness or death.

That's the way the game is played. The entities engineer the
fulfillment of a few minor predictions. And then just when men
and women are convinced that the entities know everything

about the future, they toss in a big one, and leave their trusting followers waiting on some hilltop for spaceships that never come. It's a heartless game. It has been called "the tiger behind the door of prophecy."

And that isn't all. People looking on are harmed too. They see these major predictions fail again and again. And they decide to have nothing to do with prophecy—even Bible prophecy. And that is a dangerous mistake!

Why are people taken in by these psychic hoaxes? One reason is that they do not know what the Bible teaches, though they could have known. Or they *do know* what it teaches and have rejected it. The apostle tells us that many people will be fatally deceived *because* they rejected truth. Listen: "They perish because they refused to love the truth and so be saved. For this reason God sends them a powerful delusion so that they will believe the lie." 2 Thessalonians 2:10, 11, NIV.

Now this doesn't mean that God *originates* the delusion. But when men and women definitely and finally refuse truth, God *permits* them to be overcome by Satan's powerful delusions.

A second reason people are taken in is that they believe everything supernatural is from God. Notice this: "The coming of the lawless one will be in accordance with the work of Satan displayed in all kinds of counterfeit miracles, signs and wonders." 2 Thessalonians 2:9, NIV.

The work of Satan in these last days will include all kinds of counterfeit miracles. This is what we can expect. And if we insist on thinking that all these miracles come from God, we haven't a chance!

The third reason people are taken in is that they are reckless concerning their own safety. What do I mean? Simply this: There are people who make their homes a fortress with bolts and locks. They want to protect themselves against the Hillside Strangler and the Trailside Killer and the South Hill Rapist and all the rest. But they will let demons into their homes— demons masquerading as deceased loved ones or spirit guides or spirit doctors or whatever—and let them take control of their lives without ever questioning their identity or their truthfulness. That, I say, is recklessness!

Then the fourth reason people are taken in is that they find the things taught by demons more attractive than truth. The apostle Paul wrote to Timothy, "The Spirit clearly says that in later times some will abandon the faith and follow deceiving spirits and things taught by demons." 1 Timothy 4:1, NIV.

They find truth uninteresting. And truth asks for a commitment. In contrast, they find it exciting to think they are communicating with deceased loved ones or space people. And the teachings of demons make no demands of them—except the surrender of their minds and a lifetime of bondage. But they find that out too late!

Just what do demons teach? What are the doctrines of devils? Spiritism teaches

1. that it is possible to communicate with the dead;
2. that man will never die, that he is immortal and cannot die;
3. that man can become like God, or even become God, that there is divinity within each of us;
4. that there is no future judgment;
5. that at death everybody goes to the same good place, wherever that may be, regardless of how he or she has lived;
6. that in future lives there will be opportunity to correct the wrongs done in this one.

There they are—the telltale marks of the fallen angel's teaching. Easy to recognize. If you're alert.

Well, what does the fallen angel have in mind? What is all his propaganda leading up to? I think you will see.

In May, 1967, a man named Knud Weiking, in Denmark, began receiving a series of telepathic messages which included several prophecies that came true. Then he was told to build a lead-lined bomb shelter and prepare for a holocaust on December 24. He did. He and his friends managed to complete the $30,000 shelter in about three weeks. On December 24 they locked themselves in their bomb shelter and waited.

The Danish cult was not alone, however, in being apprehensive about December 24. Mediums and sensitives and UFO contactees throughout the world were getting identical messages. Something unprecedented was going to happen on that date. At midnight a great light would appear in the sky—and that would be it!

After December 24 had passed, the American press ridiculed the Danish cult for being taken in. But Knud Weiking had an explanation. He said he had received this message: "I told you two thousand years ago that a time would be given and even so I would not come. If you had read your Bible a little more carefully, you would have borne in mind the story of the bridegroom who did not come at the time he was expected. Be watchful so that you are not found without oil in your lamps. I have told you I will come with suddenness, and I shall be coming soon."

Is that what the fallen angel is up to? Does he have in mind pulling off a second coming of his own—ahead of the real one—complete with a phony Christ and phony angels? Are they doing some practice runs to see how their network is operating? Is that what the UFO entities are rehearsing for—the big one to come?

It could be!

Remember Dr. Laughead and his followers, waiting for the end of the world?

And remember those twenty people who disappeared from an Oregon town—because they were promised a trip by UFO to a better world?

There have been others. And there most certainly will be more!

But listen! What we are witnessing, and what is happening behind the scenes, involves far more than UFOs. It's the entities back of the UFOs. It's all of spiritism. It's the whole occult world!

It's possible that UFOs may play no part at all in the counterfeiting of Christ and His second coming. I don't know. But I do know Christ will be impersonated. And it would surprise me if UFOs were not involved in some way. It's difficult to see why the enemy would engineer all this conditioning of millions of people if he didn't intend to move in and turn the popular interest in extraterrestrials to his own ends.

The fallen angel has been in this impersonation game for

thousands of years. He has impersonated dead people and living people and space people. Don't you think he'll go for the big one? Don't you think he'll impersonate Jesus too? Worship is what he is after. That's the name of the treacherous game he is playing!

Ellen White describes in *The Great Controversy*, page 624, the impersonation of Christ as if she were an eyewitness. Listen:

"As the crowning act in the great drama of deception, Satan himself will personate Christ. The church has long professed to look to the Saviour's advent as the consummation of her hopes. Now the great deceiver will make it appear that Christ has come. In different parts of the earth, Satan will manifest himself among men as a majestic being of dazzling brightness, resembling the description of the Son of God given by John in the Revelation.... The glory that surrounds him is unsurpassed by anything that mortal eyes have yet beheld. The shout of triumph rings out upon the air: 'Christ has come! Christ has come!' The people prostrate themselves in adoration before him, while he lifts up his hands and pronounces a blessing upon them, as Christ himself blessed His disciples when He was upon the earth. His voice is soft and subdued, yet full of melody. In gentle, compassionate tones he presents some of the same gracious, heavenly truths which the Saviour uttered; he heals the diseases of the people, and then, in his assumed character of Christ, he claims to have changed the [law of God]. . . . This is the strong, almost overmastering delusion."

Do you see what is coming? Do you see where the world is being led? Do you see the monstrous hoax for which millions are being subtly conditioned?

The rebel chief may let some of his helpers play savior now—in the rehearsals. But when his extravaganza goes on for real, you can be sure he won't leave the starring role to others. He'll play it himself. It's he who wants the worship. And he'll get it. Almost the whole world will bow down to a masquerading Satan—believing him to be Christ!

What a tragedy that millions upon millions will have neglected the Book that would have saved them, will have tampered with the enemy's tricks, will have become involved with his phony phenomena, will have voluntarily submitted their minds and bodies to his control—until it all ends at the feet of a masquerading impostor! And there will be no way back!

Remember Francis Gary Powers—shot down over Russia in the U-2 incident? He survived that. Years later he was piloting a news helicopter for NBC television in Los Angeles. It was a bad year for fires. He and his cameraman were covering the big Santa Barbara fire. Flying in and out of the canyons, they were excited about the fantastic pictures they had for the five-o'clock news. So excited that the condition of their own fuel tank was forgotten. They crashed in a plowed field two miles from the airport—and both men were dead!

Friend, never was it more important to be alert and aware of what the fallen angel is doing. To be uninformed is to be in peril. But even with the right information wouldn't it be a tragedy if we were to become so absorbed in watching the enemy's strange, hypnotic fires that we forget the state of our own relationship with the Lord Jesus—the Source of all power? We are so near the airport, so near our final landing. It would be stupid to lose out now. Our only safety is in being *aware* of the fallen angel—but *in love* with Jesus!

The Spectacular Finish

God must love the spectacular. He splashes His paints across the evening sky and creates the beauty we frame. He makes a sea out of glass—to reflect the bold and breathless colors of His throne. He builds His streets out of gold instead of concrete. He calls upon the wind, with a touch of lightning and the crashing cymbals of His thunder—to be His overture. He has more galaxies than any computer can count. And I wonder if He leaves one empty just for fireworks—for His pleasure and ours.

But the greatest spectaculars of all He tucks into places like very dark days—and human hearts. And then He turns back to planning the spectacular finish of what we call time. Because He'll be needing it before long!

It was June 14, 1975.

Murray and Roslyn Hughes, eight years old and six, were in the back seats of the plane—their shoes off and their seatbelts tight—when it crashed in a remote section of the Australian Outback. They were not hurt. But their father slumped unconscious in the pilot seat, and their mother was pinned in the cockpit.

Murray couldn't forget the desperation in his mother's voice as she cried, "Take Rossie and go get help! Don't stop for anything!"

The children couldn't find their shoes, so they started out without them. And for twelve hours they stumbled barefoot down the snake-infested mountainside, thinking only of their broken and bleeding parents up there in the fog-enshrouded forest.

Again and again they prayed, "Please, God, make us brave!"

A rancher spotted them in a pasture seven miles from the wreckage. He said, "They were just babies. I couldn't believe it when I saw them out there." They were shivering from the cold, their clothes in tatters. They were badly scratched up, and their feet were bleeding.

"The little girl was very brave," said the rancher, "clutching a small purse with a brush and comb inside. The boy came up and told me to get help for his mother and father. He was the bravest boy I'd ever come across. His feet were cut up real bad, but he didn't want to rest. He had just one thought in mind—to get help for his parents."

The organizer of the rescue party said, "You may think twelve hours isn't long. But this is the toughest country there is. It's dense forest, and the bush is alive with deadly snakes and poisonous spiders. I don't think those two kids could have survived very much longer out there."

Roslyn told about their ordeal. She said, "Mommy told us to be brave and go for help. It was very misty and we couldn't see where we were going. The trees had big roots sticking out of the ground and I kept tripping over them.

"The ground was very rough," she said. "Mommy told us to take our shoes off in the plane so that we would be more comfortable, and when the crash happened we couldn't find them. It hurt when we walked on the ground. There were rough stones and I kept stubbing my toes."

And she went on, "We were very scared. We kept hearing rustling noises all around us. Once, there was a very loud rustling in the bushes right next to us. I screamed. Murray was very brave. He put his arm around me, and said, 'Don't worry. I won't let anything hurt you.' "

Murray said, "I was very scared, but I didn't want Rossie to know. I just kept thinking about Mommy and Daddy and how we had to get help. I have never walked so far. The worst part was having no shoes. . . . Every now and then Rossie would stop and cry. Sometimes I would let her lie down for a while."

The rescue party was too late. And Murray wept, "I only wish we could tell Mommy and Daddy we tried our best!"

How like what Jesus did! People He had made, on a planet He had made, were in trouble. Without help they couldn't survive. And He said, "I'll go, Father." And the Father said, "Go, Son. And don't stop for anything!"

He left His crown behind. It would have been easier with His crown—so much easier. But He didn't stop for anything. All He could think of was finding help—finding a way to save you and me. And again and again He prayed, "Father, make Me brave!"

And so He came to Bethlehem!

When He was twelve years old He visited the magnificent temple. For the first time He saw the priests offering innocent lambs on the altar. He was fascinated by what He saw. There was something mysterious about it—something that seemed to be tied to His own life. And then suddenly He understood. Now it was clear to Him. He Himself was to be the Lamb. He Himself was to be the innocent Sacrifice for men's sins. He Himself was the Way to save a lost race. That's why He had come!

And so He kept straight on to Calvary. All He could think of was men and women who were lost. He had to go on. He was the Lamb!

We have a choice as to how the story ends. It can end with you and me slumped in the cockpit of a wrecked planet. Or it can end in the most spectacular rescue of all time—if we are willing!

But when it's all over, when the last man has made his choice, and when millions have chosen to go down with this planet, I seem to hear the Saviour saying, "Father, I just wish I could tell them I tried My best!"

Is it possible that we are confused about what is really spectacular? The cross of Calvary is the most spectacular event of all time. It's God's incredible exhibit before the court of the universe. It's His unanswerable answer to the charges of those— Satan first among them—who said He didn't care!

If you want the spectacular, you won't have to wait long. God will soon oblige. God is letting Satan do his miracles first. Then God will do His. And Satan's, in comparison, will look like silly tricks!

No words can describe the day when God takes over. Our

boasted megatons will seem like popping corn when God takes the affairs of this earth in hand. And Satan can only stand by and watch—helpless, amazed, and terrified!

The fallen angel with his toys can stop a few motors. But God can stop history! Satan can set compasses spinning. But God can defy gravity and lift His people into the sky—and take them home! Satan's UFOs can scorch a little piece of earth. But God can set the mountains smoking with His presence! Satan can bring fire from heaven to deceive men. But God, with fire, can destroy the earth and make it new again! Satan can trace a mysterious image on a piece of film. But God can trace His own image on human hearts! Satan can cause the personality to deteriorate. But God can make men new. And transformed lives are the greatest miracle of all!

The life of the trusting Christian is one constant spectacular. It is a succession of miracles. And God's clock is precisely accurate. He is never late. No emergency takes Him by surprise!

We don't have to worry about God's timing. Over and over it has been demonstrated that His providence can tread safely over circumstances so precarious that the slightest wind could blow a traveler off course, where just a word left unsaid, a seemingly trivial matter neglected, could block the divine plan. How do I know? Because I've seen it—personally—times without number!

Wouldn't you like to have been watching the day God stepped out into space and called our world into existence? He just spoke the word. And there it was! See Psalm 33:6, 9. And then He hung it out into space—on nothing! See Job 26:7.

I like the colorful way Dr. Shadrack Meshack Lockridge pictures it. Listen:

"Standing on nothing, He reached out where there was nowhere to reach and caught something when there was nothing to catch, and hung something on nothing, and told it to stay there. . . . Standing on nothing He took the hammer of His own will, and He struck the anvil of His omnipotence and sparks flew therefrom and He caught them on the tips of His fingers and flung them out into space and bedecked the heavens with stars!"

However God did it, it was a spectacular for sure!

And then there was the Flood of Noah's day. Nothing we've ever experienced can qualify us to understand what happened. Water coming from the clouds in mighty cataracts. Water gushing forth from the earth. Lightning tearing across the sky. Mountains rising and falling. Wind and fire and volcanoes. Tidal waves. The earth torn and twisted and convulsed. A negative spectacular that left only eight people alive!

I was about to say that you and I may have grandstand seats for the spectacular windup of history—the return of Jesus to this earth. But that is hardly correct. There won't be any grandstand seats. There won't be any spectators. Because every man, woman, and child will be personally involved, and the nature of that involvement is up to the individual!

With words borrowed from an inspired pen, let me picture that day:

"It is at midnight that God manifests His power for the deliverance of His people. The sun appears, shining in its strength. Signs and wonders follow in quick succession. The wicked look with terror and amazement upon the scene, while the righteous behold with solemn joy the tokens of their deliverance. Everything in nature seems turned out of its course. The streams cease to flow. Dark, heavy clouds come up and clash against each other. In the midst of the angry heavens is one clear space of indescribable glory, whence comes the voice of God like the sound of many waters, saying 'It is done.'

"That voice shakes the heavens and the earth. There is a mighty earthquake. . . . The firmament appears to open and shut. The glory from the throne of God seems flashing through. The mountains shake like a reed in the wind, and ragged rocks are scattered on every side. There is a roar as of a coming tempest. The sea is lashed into fury. There is heard the shriek of the hurricane like the voice of demons upon a mission of destruction. The whole earth heaves and swells like the waves of the sea. Its surface is breaking up. Its very foundations seem to be giving way. Mountain chains are sinking. Inhabited islands disappear. The seaports that have become like Sodom for wickedness are swallowed up by the angry waters. . . . Great hailstones, every one 'about the weight of a talent [about a hundred pounds]' are doing their work of destruction. . . . The proudest cities of the earth are laid low. . . .

"Fierce lightnings leap from the heavens, enveloping the earth in a sheet of flame. Above the terrific roar of thunder, voices, mysterious and awful, declare the doom of the wicked. . . . Those who a little before were so reckless, so boastful and defiant . . . are now overwhelmed with consternation and shuddering in fear. Their wails are heard above the sound of the elements. Demons acknowledge the deity of Christ and tremble before His power, while men are supplicating for mercy and groveling in abject terror. . . .

"Through a rift in the clouds there beams a star whose brilliancy is increased fourfold in contrast with the darkness. It speaks hope and joy to the faithful, but severity and wrath to the transgressors of God's law. . . .

"Soon there appears in the east a small black cloud, about half the size of a man's hand. It is the cloud which surrounds the Saviour and which seems in the distance to be shrouded in darkness. The people of God know this to be the sign of the Son of man. In solemn silence they gaze upon it as it draws nearer the earth, becoming lighter and more glorious, until it is a great white cloud, its base a glory like consuming fire, and above it the rainbow of the covenant. Jesus rides forth as a mighty conqueror. . . . With anthems of celestial melody the holy angels, a vast, unnumbered throng, attend Him on His way. . . . No human pen can portray the scene; no mortal mind is adequate to conceive its splendor."—*The Great Controversy,* pp. 636-641.

A scene spectacular beyond words!

But listen. The cross of Calvary is even more spectacular than the return of Jesus to this earth. His return to this planet can be understood. Calvary never can. Not fully. Not by men. Not by angels. Not by the residents of unfallen worlds!

Calvary! The most tragic day of all history. Men nailing their Creator to a cross! But it was also a day for great rejoicing. Men didn't know what was happening that day. But angels did. When they heard the Son of God cry out from the cross, "It is finished!" they knew its significance for all the universe. Jesus had reached the finish line. He had fallen dead across it. But He had reached it. Without sinning once. Not one temptation, not one test of His faith or His patience, not one trick of the enemy, had left the slightest taint upon Him. He was a perfect Saviour!

But the men He had come to save—didn't want to be saved!

Imagine—if you can—what a scandalous tragedy it would have been if Murray and Roslyn had stumbled down that treacherous mountainside as they did, and the rescue party had reached their parents in time—only to be told that they didn't want to be rescued. After all it had cost to make rescue possible!

But that's what some of us are doing to our Lord!

He went through infinitely more than those two devoted children. He walked through serpent-infested country for thirty-three years—and went home to His Father with His hands and His feet scarred for eternity by the daring rescue attempt. Will we tell Him we don't want to be rescued after all?

Thirty-three years! And He never turned back. Sometimes He was so weary, so faint and exhausted, so crushed by it all, that the angels let Him rest a few moments in their arms. But He kept thinking of you and me—and He had to go on. He was the Lamb of God. And He had an appointment with a rough and rugged cross outside Jerusalem. A cross that should have been yours. And mine!

Friend, it's perfectly safe to let Jesus capture your heart!

Goodbyes Don't Have to Be Final

Rising from this troubled planet like an incense of doom is the persistent question, Why? It's the heartcry of millions. This earth, as God sees it, is not a riot of color and song. It is a symphony of tears.

Doesn't God care? Is He unconcerned about this world being the cemetery of the universe? Are we only a forgotten cinder out on the edge of an unimportant galaxy? A world that doesn't matter?

On one of my visits to the old city of Jerusalem I was shown the place where it is believed that Abraham once stood with his son Isaac atop the mountain. I tried to picture it. There stood Abraham, his knife raised, ready to give up all he had for his God. And then an angel stayed his hand.

Fifteen centuries later, almost on that very spot, the God of the universe watched His own Son die. And there was no angel to stay the hand of death. No vice to cry out, "It is enough!"

Was it that way with you when you read the story? Did you hope till the last that the hand of death would be restrained? Only to be finally disappointed?

I say it reverently, you and God have something in common now. The cross He has given to you is one that He first bore Himself.

Yes, you can never look at Calvary and say He doesn't care—He doesn't understand!

And so I want to bring you hope and comfort from an ancient and often neglected Book. But I bring you even more than that. I bring you a Person!

You see, you have lost a person. Nothing but a person can fill the place left empty.

Oh, it's one thing to be strong when a companion shares the load. But it's quite another thing to push on when you can no longer feel the lift on the other side of the yoke.

I bring you a Person. That Person is Jesus Christ. David knew Him. He said, "Yea, though I walk through the valley of the shadow of death, I will fear no evil: for thou art with me." Psalm 23:4, KJV.

And God said through Isaiah, "When you pass through the waters, I will be with you; and through the rivers, they will not overflow you. When you walk through the fire, you will not be scorched, nor will the flame burn you." Isaiah 43:2, NASB.

Can't you trust a God like that?

Grief, you see, is sometimes so violent in its attack that we are tempted to reach out to stay God's hand. But don't friend. Don't!

Said the poet,

> Don't touch His hand!
> A Master Artist paints.
> What you have thought to do
> Would only blur the picture
> That He makes.
> You cannot see
> That which His mind intends
> To make of you.
> Your awkward touch might easily
> Upset the colors, and the easel too.
> Don't touch what He is doing.
> You fear that He might spoil it all
> Unless you hold Him back.
> But wait!
> Don't touch His hand!
> For He is God—
> And He is wise—
> And He is love!

Yes, wait! You can trust a God like that!

One day we shall see that sorrow is sometimes only the veil with which God covers His glory as He stands close by. Where now we see only confusion and loss and broken patterns, then we shall see perfect and beautiful harmony. We shall see, one day soon, that God knows best how to answer prayer!

I discover that there is far more than sympathy in the Word of God. Jesus did not say, "Blessed are they that mourn," and then pass by on the other side. He met death head on—and did something about it!

Watch Him as He walks nineteen hundred years ago along a rocky path outside a little Palestine village. Approaching Him, moving slowly along the cobblestone street and out through the gate, is a funeral procession. A mother walks beside the now still form of the son who has been her pride and her support.

Jesus and the grieving mother are about to meet. Will He stop to offer her comfort? More than that. He calls the son to life and restores him to his mother.

Jesus was like that. His love was stronger than death. No one ever died in His presence. No one could.

Lazarus could never have died if Jesus had been at His side. His sisters knew that. That's why each kept saying, "Lord, if You had been here, my brother would not have died."

But now, four days after death had dealt its blow, Jesus had come to cheer the sorrowing sisters. How would He do it? How would He deal with death? What would He say to bring comfort in an hour like this?

He said simply, "Your brother will rise again."

And Martha understood. She knew what He meant. They had talked of these things before. And she replied, "I know that he will rise again in the resurrection at the last day."

The resurrection at the last day. That is the hope of the Scriptures. There is no better news in all the Book than those simple words, "Your brother will rise again."

But He couldn't wait. Jesus couldn't wait. He was like that. He chose to demonstrate then and there what the resurrection would be like. He called out, "Lazarus, come forth!" And he came forth!

Yes, Jesus continually urged His followers to look beyond

this life, to look beyond this day. And then, in one of the most profound and miraculous demonstrations of all time, He laid down His own life—and after three days walked out of the tomb!

At that moment the power of death was broken. And now, for the first time in human history, there surged in man's breast the living conviction that his fondest hope, cherished so long, had at last been made certain. Our dead could be seen and loved again!

The prophet Isaiah, long centuries before, had said it: "Thy dead men shall live, together with my dead body shall they arise. . . . And the earth shall cast out the dead." Isaiah 26:19, KJV.

"Thy dead men shall live." Doesn't that mean, Your dead too shall live? Wonderful news!

Isaiah had declared it a possibility. But Jesus demonstrated it!

Let me ask you, Do you believe that Jesus rose from the dead? Of course you do, if you are a Christian.

Then remember this. The resurrection of your loved one is as certain as the resurrection of Christ!

But someone is saying, "This is all so wonderful. But this is not for me. You see, my son, my daughter, did not believe."

I ask you, How do you know?

I think of a mother who did her best to train her boy in the right way. But he turned out to be a thief. And at last he was executed for his crime. His was one of three crosses on a hill outside Jerusalem.

His mother may well have stood by weeping, her sobs caught up in the noise of the crowd. She may not have heard her son's words as he turned in those last moments to the One dying at his side and said, "Lord, remember me when You come into Your kingdom." She may never have known.

Don't be too sure, then, that someone dear to you is without hope. Can you not leave it in God's hands? You too can turn to the Scriptures and share in their comfort and their hope. Listen to this: "For the Lord himself will come down from heaven, with a loud command, with the voice of the archangel and with the trumpet call of God, and the dead in Christ will rise first. After that, we who are still alive and are left will be caught up with them in the clouds to meet the Lord in the air. And so we will be with the Lord forever. Therefore encourage each other with these words." 1 Thessalonians 4:16-18, NIV.

I ask you, Could there be any better news—any better encouragement?

Picture it if you can. The Son of God piercing the vaulted heavens, moving down the star-studded procession way of the skies, attended by myriads of angels. And then He calls out with a voice of thunder, "Wake up! Wake up to everlasting life!" And *your dead too* will hear!

That voice calling the loved ones we have lost will be heard the world around. Families will be reunited. Children snatched away by death will be placed again in their mother's arms. What a reunion day!

What does this mean to you? What does it mean to me? It means that there is something better beyond this day. It means that death is on the way out!

Think for a moment. Think what that day will mean to the crippled, to the blind, to those weakened by disease, to minds confused by fear. God says, "The eyes of the blind shall be opened, and the ears of the deaf shall be unstopped. Then shall the lame man leap. . . , and the tongue of the dumb sing." Isaiah 35:5, 6, KJV.

But think what it will mean to the able-bodied and the strong, to those who love life and want to live. You see, death may even seem welcome to a body ravaged by disease and pain. But to the strong and youthful, death can mean only disappointed hopes, disillusionment, shattered ambitions.

But here is the answer to death's sting. Not in the discoveries of science, not in the exploration of outer space, not in anything man can do, but in the promise of the resurrection made by One who Himself demonstrated its possibility—here is our hope!

I find an intriguing parallel in the story of one of the most significant battles in world history—that of the Duke of Wellington and Napoleon Bonaparte. The old verger of Winchester Cathedral never tired of telling the story of the day when the news of the battle reached England. It came by sailing vessel to the south coast and was carried overland by semaphore to the top of Winchester Cathedral and on to London.

The people eagerly waited as the semaphore spelled out the words:

"W-E-L-L-I-N-G-T-O-N   D-E-F-E-A-T-E-D."

Just then a dense fog settled down over the harbor, as this incomplete message was waved on to London. A pall of gloom and discouragement settled over the land. Streets were barricaded. Women and the elderly prepared to defend their country in the streets and in the fields if necessary. But finally the fog lifted, and the semaphore signals came through again:

"W-E-L-L-I-N-G-T-O-N D-E-F-E-A-T-E-D T-H-E E-N-E-M-Y."

Can you imagine the wild delirium of joy that spread like a prairie fire, made all the more exhilarating when contrasted with the earlier news?

Need I draw the parallel? Doesn't this experience illustrate the meaning that the disciples read into Christ's crucifixion?

The sun refused to shine on the scene. Darkness covered the earth. The resounding peals of thunder reduced the slender faith of the disciples to just two words:

"J-E-S-U-S   D-E-F-E-A-T-E-D."

As friends laid His limp, lifeless body in a borrowed tomb, the disciples' depression deepened. Hear them reasoning, "We trusted that it had been He which should have redeemed Israel." They thought they had made a mistake. Surely Jesus must not be the long-awaited Saviour after all.

But then as the light broke on that resurrection morning, the message which should have been understood by His closest followers began to be clarified. And the world has ever since been able to read the life-giving and glorious message:

"J-E-S-U-S   D-E-F-E-A-T-E-D   D-E-A-T-H."

I ask you, Is there any better news? Tongue cannot tell it, pen cannot write it—the hope this completed message brings to the human breast. Take courage, friend. There is hope beyond this day. Its goodbyes are not as final as you thought. For on the resurrection morning your loved ones too will live!

The Ultimate Hoax

Suppose, if you will, that you meet an impostor who has decided to stage a counterfeit second coming—a counterfeit return of Christ to this planet. Just what would he have to do?

Now I know, as you know, that it isn't difficult to get a following these days. Some people seem to have no difficulty in attracting millions. With Bible literacy low and gullibility high, even a Jonestown is not impossible. In fact, it was relatively easy.

So let me reword my question. *What would an impostor have to do to fool the man who knows his Bible?*

First of all, of course, he would need someone to play the role of Christ. And that isn't difficult, because Satan himself would be glad to volunteer. He's been practicing up for just such a role for millenniums.

Could Satan disguise himself sufficiently? Could he make himself *look* anything like Christ? Could he make himself *sound* enough like Christ to fool even a Bible-reading Christian? Absolutely. The apostle Paul says that "Satan himself is transformed into an angel of light." 2 Corinthians 11:14, KJV.

And if he needs some miracles, remember that, according to the book of Revelation, demons can work miracles. See Revelation 16:14.

So far it's easy.

But wait. So far we've only seen that it would not be difficult for Satan and his demons to set up a hoax that would fool millions. But our question is this: What would an impostor have to

143

do, what would Satan have to do, to duplicate exactly the Bible description of the second coming of Christ?

Satan has a lot of power, supernatural power. He can disguise himself. He can impersonate. He can work miracles. He can fool people. But his power is limited. He can go only so far.

Listen. If any impostor, even Satan himself, wants to successfully duplicate the return of Christ, he will have to be able to get up there in the sky and descend to earth in the clouds of heaven. Because Jesus said, "They shall see the Son of man coming in the clouds of heaven with power and great glory." Matthew 24:30, KJV.

Now it isn't so easy. Now it's getting tough. But let's go on.

An impostor would have to get the cooperation of all the angels of heaven, every one of them. Because they're all descending to earth along with Christ. See Matthew 25:31.

Do you think the loyal angels of heaven would ever cooperate with a rebel impostor?

But it gets more difficult as we go along. We read this about the second coming: "Look, he is coming with the clouds, and every eye will see him, even those who pierced him; and all the peoples of the earth will mourn because of him." Revelation 1:7, NIV.

Here are insurmountable problems for any impostor. It says that every eye will see Jesus as He returns. Everybody will be watching. Nobody will have to be told what is happening—or hear it on the news. And that means everybody everywhere on earth, because it says that all the peoples of the earth will be involved.

Just how our God will make it possible for everyone on earth, not only east and west but north and south as well—just how God will make it possible for everyone on earth to see what is happening, I don't know. It would seem that some manipulation of the planet itself, some turning or twirling of the globe, must be involved. Would any impostor be able to manage that?

And there's something else in the verse we just read. It says that those who crucified Jesus will see Him return in glory. This would require a resurrection of those people. It would mean bringing forth from their graves those who played a special part in the death of Jesus. Could an impostor do that?

An impostor, if he is to really duplicate the second coming, would have to have the cooperation of nature. For listen to this: "Out of the temple came a loud voice from the throne, saying, 'It is done!' Then there came flashes of lightning, rumblings, peals of thunder and a severe earthquake. No earthquake like it has ever occurred since man has been on earth, so tremendous was the quake. . . . And the cities of the nations collapsed. . . . Every island fled away and the mountains could not be found. From the sky huge hailstones of about a hundred pounds each fell upon men." Revelation 16:17-21, NIV.

Would any impostor have the power to do all this?

But there is still more. Here is the apostle Paul's description of the second coming: "For the Lord himself will come down from heaven, with a loud command, with the voice of the archangel and with the trumpet call of God, and the dead in Christ will rise first. After that, we who are still alive and are left will be caught up with them into the clouds to meet the Lord in the air. And so we will be with the Lord forever." 1 Thessalonians 4:16, 17, NIV.

Will any impostor be able to break open the graves all around the earth and call to life those who have died trusting in their Lord? Never!

And did you notice that the feet of Jesus, when He returns, will not even touch the ground? He comes no nearer than the living cloud of angels that escort Him. To be sure, He comes very near the earth—near enough for His voice to be heard by all, near enough to call the dead to life. But He does not actually set foot on the ground. *Remember this* when you hear on the evening news that Christ has returned and is out in the Arizona desert. *Remember this* when you hear that Jesus is working miracles in Times Square. *Remember this* when you hear that a being believed to be Jesus Christ has just stepped out of a UFO!

Do you see how terribly important it is to know *how* Jesus is going to return? It's our *only guarantee* against being fatally deceived!

Jesus warned that there would be many impostors, many

false Christs. And He said they would work great signs and wonders—miracles—so that if possible even His own people would be deceived. See Matthew 24:24. But He added, "So if anyone tells you, 'There he is, out in the desert,' do not go out; or, 'Here he is, in the inner rooms,' do not believe it." Matthew 24:26, NIV.

You say, "Don't we have to check these things out? Don't we have to go and listen so we can decide whether it's Jesus or not?"

No. Jesus is saying to us, "Look! You don't need to bother with checking out all these people who claim to be Christ—no matter how many miracles they work, no matter how many millions may follow them. Because I have told you just *how* I will return. So you won't need to pay any attention to anyone who appears some other way."

There's not much of anything that Satan won't try—if it has any chance at all of serving his evil purposes. I believe he definitely will try to impersonate Christ and counterfeit the second coming. I believe he will do it for four reasons—at least four:

1. He knows that most people haven't read the Bible enough to know—and remember—*how* Jesus will return.

2. He knows that among those who do read and study the Bible there are many who, at his satanic instigation, have simply been playing games with Bible prophecy—with the book of Revelation especially. They are weaving for themselves a fabric of speculation and wishful thinking. They have figured out how they would like future events to be—and have convinced themselves that that's the way it will be. In spite of all the scriptures that describe the second coming as the most spectacular event since creation, some have decided that it will really be a secret affair that only a few will be aware of. And some are expecting things to happen in Israel that won't happen in Israel. And some believe Christ will set up a political kingdom on this earth in the near future. And some, influenced by the psychics, have decided Jesus will return in 1999 and that therefore we all have plenty of time to prepare. If only we would let the Bible be its own interpreter! How much safer we would be! One thing is certain. The future is not going to happen a thou-

sand different ways. It will happen only *one way*—the way the Bible describes!

3. Satan knows that with his supernatural power, the impersonation will be so spectacular, so convincing, *so like Jesus* that it will be impossible by the senses alone to detect the counterfeit.

4. The fallen angel is so desperate, so determined to gain the worship of men and women one way or another—even if only for an hour and even if by mistake—that he will go ahead with his plan even though he knows that any successes will be of very short duration. His plea to the human race, as it was to Jesus in the wilderness temptation, is this: "Worship me just once. Worship me just a little—even if you don't mean it!"

And the tragedy is that when the Lord Jesus appears in the sky, almost everybody will already have bowed down to a masquerade impostor, believing him to be Christ!

We are being conditioned for a monstrous deception that will sweep the world—a deception tailored to fit the mood of this space-minded generation. Unquestionably Satan is planning some sort of end-of-the-world extravaganza in which he will play the leading role.

And don't ever think that the big hoax will be easy to ignore. On the contrary, it will be so cleverly carried out as to be almost overpowering. Satan and his angels-turned-demons have been in this impersonating business for thousands of years. They have impersonated angels. They have impersonated dead people. They have impersonated living people. They have impersonated people from outer space. Why not go for the big one? Why not impersonate Jesus—the second coming and all? After all, Satan has always wanted Jesus' place!

Already we have witnessed a number of dry runs—rehearsals for Satan's second-coming stunt. People locking themselves in a lead-lined bomb shelter and waiting for the end of the world. People gathering on a mountaintop, expecting to be picked up by a spaceship. People selling their homes and abandoning their families, following a leader somewhere—only to be disillusioned. The world is a pushover for a counterfeit Christ—for anyone who appears able to solve our problems that are getting out of hand. The world is wired for the big hoax!

Satan has permitted his followers to stand in for him in these rehearsals. But you can be assured that when he is ready for the big show, he will play the starring role himself. And few will escape fatal deception—only those who have learned to trust the Scriptures more than their eyes and ears!

Ellen White, many years ago, described the day of the ultimate hoax. Listen:

"As the crowning act in the great drama of deception, Satan himself will personate Christ. . . . Now the great deceiver will make it appear that Christ has come. In different parts of the earth, Satan will manifest himself among men as a majestic being of dazzling brightness, resembling the description of the Son of God given by John in the Revelation. . . . The glory that surrounds him is unsurpassed by anything that mortal eyes have yet beheld. The shout of triumph rings out upon the air: 'Christ has come! Christ has come!' The people prostrate themselves in adoration before him, while he lifts up his hands and pronounces a blessing upon them, as Christ blessed His disciples when He was upon the earth. His voice is soft and subdued, yet full of melody. In gentle, compassionate tones he presents some of the same gracious, heavenly truths which the Saviour uttered; he heals the diseases of the people, and then, in his assumed character of Christ, he claims to have changed the [law of God]. . . . This is the strong, almost overmastering delusion." —*The Great Controversy*, page 624.

There he stands, this being of dazzling brightness. If you ask your eyes, Who is it? Jesus. If you ask your ears, Who is it? Jesus. If you ask your feelings, Who is it? Jesus.

But if you ask the Scriptures, Who is it? A masquerading devil! And almost all the world will bow down, taken in by the ultimate hoax!

Friend, I commend to you the Word of God. Read it! Read it for your life!

Destination Life

Does the world we live in have an appointment in Samarra? Do we face annihilation by the product of our own technology? Must we look forward to collision with some speeding world? Are we threatened with invasion from outer space? Is civilization one day soon to be finished, with only a few survivors left to start again?

No. We are no longer trapped with a prognosis of fatalism. No longer must we feel the cold, meaningless chill of facing the unknown. Even a brush with the death angel need not be a frightening experience. To face death's reality need not paralyze with fear. For we know now that there is something better beyond this day.

We have an appointment to keep. But it is not in Samarra. It is not with fatalism or despair. It is not with annihilation or colliding worlds or marauders from outer space. It is not with the spirit world or its strange altars or its crystal balls. Our appointment is not with any of these. It is with life—if we choose.

In the final analysis we hold the future in our own hands. Your destination and mine is a matter of deliberate choice. We are not doomed to a death ride to Samarra. Ahead of us, spreading out across eternity, is life—if we want it.

Where is that life to be? What will it be like? Can we know?

Yes, we can. And I believe that now we are ready to appreciate the future that unfolds in the Sacred Book.

You see, we needed to settle some other matters first. We

149

needed to know something of the meaning of life, and of death, before we could understand the future. Any confusion or mis-understanding in regard to what man is must necessarily mean confusion about his destiny.

In other words, if man is nothing more than a collection of molecules, a happenstance creature evolving by trial and error through the ages, then what hope is there? The divine record is that man is made in the image of God, with a conscience. If man rejects this, what hope does he have? What future is there for a creature that arrived where he is only by accident and chance and is destined to continue his journey in the same way? If some cosmic accident brought him into being in the first place, some cosmic accident in the years ahead may destroy him.

If a man accepts these popular concepts of his own origin, the future described in Scripture is meaningless. But when he abandons these hopeless, confusing contradictions, the prospect before him opens in a panorama of hope beyond his wildest dreams.

There is good news in store. For if we have found the Book to be clear about man's origin, about what happens to him at death, we shall find it equally clear about his destiny. And I thank God that we shall not be peering into a crystal ball, or putting our faith in the shaky speculations of uncertain man. We shall have for our hope the Word of the living God.

Christian minds have long associated the future life with a place called heaven. But strangely enough, about all most people know about heaven is that it is *up* somewhere. Ask the first ten people you meet, and you will discover that the majority of men and women who have thought about it at all have no clear idea what it is like.

Heaven is up. There is no doubt about that. But to many people it is only a mixture of fairy story and imagination, with a covering of puritanic boredom that leaves it with little appeal.

In fact, the popular conception of heaven is only a little less fantastic than that pictured by a schoolboy who wrote:

"Heaven has three stories and a basement. The floor is the clouds. God sleeps on the first two floors, and Santa Claus with his reindeer and toys lives on the third floor, and the angels sleep in the basement. The houses are all made of gingerbread, and the rivers are all of different colors—red, blue, pink, green, orange. That's all."

The teacher said, "Don't those fairy stories help to develop the children's imagination, though?"

Yes, no doubt they do. But will the fairy-story idea satisfy men and women forced to take an honest look into the future?

You see, many think of heaven as a land where disembodied spirits float around in space. Or where we sit on wispy clouds playing on semi-material harps forever and ever. A place where St. Peter is supposed to go around clanking keys—which are quite material or they wouldn't clank—and letting in whom he chooses through some sort of gate into the so-called eternal bliss of the saints.

Could you imagine a more unhappy place to spend eternity than this traditional heaven? Many a successful businessman has arrived at the age of retirement only to find that retirement is what he least enjoys. To him—and to healthy, buoyant people everywhere—the prospect of passing the endless hours of eternity aimlessly strumming a harp on the edge of some cloud would be simply appalling!

These popular conceptions, or misconceptions, of heaven— picturing it as a place without purpose, with reality, without activity, without anything but endless boredom—seem so absurd, so utterly unsatisfying, that many good people have rejected the whole idea of a future life. They prefer to believe that life here and now is either heaven or hell, depending on what you make of it.

No. In the Word of the living God we shall discover that heaven is not a ghostland or a spook country. It is not a figment of the imagination. It is not a dream. It is not a filmy fiction made of harps and clouds.

Heaven, though it hangs yet beyond the reach of our telescopes, is a world as real and tangible as our own. It is not a storyland at all. The place is as real as any you have ever seen.

And the good news is this. You need not wait until our space scientists develop bigger boosters and more powerful thrust. You need not wait for our astronauts to discover heaven. The answers that men so expensively seek are already yours—in the Word of the living God.

Follow me carefully. For this thrilling possibility promises fulfillment in your day and mine—long before men with their speediest scientific achievement could be ready for anything but the most primitive space travel.

We begin with the majestic, now familiar words of the apostle Paul: "For the Lord himself shall descend from heaven with a shout, with the voice of the archangel, and with the trump of God: and the dead in Christ shall rise first: then we which are alive and remain shall be caught up together with them in the clouds, to meet the Lord in the air: and so shall we ever be with the Lord." 1 Thessalonians 4:16, 17, KJV.

No rockets. No oxygen tanks. No space suits. But gravity will be powerless to hold back the King of glory as He lifts His people through the skies. Nature's laws are His laws. The Creator is in control.

I like to think what that trip will be like. It seems reasonable that there might be stops at other worlds along the way—worlds that have never rebelled against their Creator. And then the glorious climax as the Saviour swings wide the gates of the city and welcomes us home.

Would you like to read a description of the city? Read at your leisure the entire twenty-first and twenty-second chapters of Revelation. But notice now these verses of chapter 21:

Verse 12. It has a wall. Verse 13. It has gates. Verse 14. It has foundations. Verse 15. It has measurements.

It is a city as real and as literal as any we have ever known. And the throne of God is there. The tree of life is there. There is no night, no death, no pain. And there are no tears.

But did you know that heaven, as real and satisfying as it is, is not to be our permanent home? Jesus said, "Blessed are the meek: for they shall inherit the earth." Matthew 5:5, KJV.

The meek shall inherit *the earth*. Yes, we shall not spend eternity on some cloud on the rim of the universe, or even in heaven, tangible as it is. God gave His Son that this world might forever be the home of the saved.

You see, this earth was meant to be our home. "For thus saith the Lord that created the heavens; God himself that formed the earth and made it; he hath established it, he created it not in vain, he formed it to be inhabited." Isaiah 45:18, KJV.

This world was wrested from its original owners. But God gave His Son to buy back not only a lost race but also a lost planet—a world originally intended to be man's home.

I ask you, Would our Saviour, the Son of the eternal God, consent to suffer, to bleed, to die so that you might live on some mystic cloud in a thin, vapory, immaterial existence that you would not want anyway? Hardly!

The meek shall inherit the earth. True, the meek are not in possession of much of it now. Much of it is in the hands of finance companies. But God promised it to the meek.

You ask, "Who are the meek?"

The scripture answers your question. "And the Lord said unto Abram, after that Lot was separated from him, Lift up now thine eyes, and look from the place where thou art northward, and southward, and eastward, and westward: for all the land which thou seest, to thee will I give it, and to thy seed forever." Genesis 13:14, 15, KJV.

All the land that he could see. Romans 4:13 tells us that Abraham was to be "the heir of the world."

Someone says, "The Jews are certainly fortunate. Abraham was the father of the Hebrew race. But I am a Gentile. Where do I come in?"

Listen! "And if ye be Christ's, then are ye Abraham's seed, and heirs according to the promise." Galatians 3:29, KJV.

There you have it. If you belong to Christ, then you are an heir to the original promise—an heir to this world.

Now, this world at present might not be a very desirable gift. But God will give it to His people as a perfect gift, renovated and changed and new.

"But the day of the Lord will come as a thief in the night; in the which the heavens shall pass away with a great noise, and the elements shall melt with fervent heat, the earth also and the works that are therein shall be burned up." 2 Peter 3:10, KJV.

But notice what follows: "Nevertheless we, according to his

promise, look for new heavens and a new earth, wherein dwelleth righteousness." Verse 13, KJV.

The world is imperfect now. But in the great day of the Lord, the day toward which all creation is moving, the earth will be cleansed, it will be changed, it will be made new.

A thousand happy years will have passed quickly—years spent in a real and literal heaven. Years spent with the Saviour, spent in companionship with the angels and unfallen beings from other worlds, spent in becoming acquainted with the wonders of God's universe. What a day for the scientist, the astronomer, the space traveler!

And then the hour will come for the space trip of the ages. There will be no frantic last-minute countdown, no hurried repairing of spaceship doors that might leak precious oxygen out into space, no fear of radiation belts.

Visualize, if you can, this most unusual drama ever enacted. The entire city, the New Jerusalem, preceded by all its inhabitants, with the throne of God and with the tree of life, moves safely out into space and begins its long journey. I like to picture it moving down through the star-lined corridor of Orion, that giant cavern in the skies. Its destination—earth!

"And I saw a new heaven and a new earth: for the first heaven and the first earth were passed away; and there was no more sea. And I John saw the Holy City, New Jerusalem, coming down from God out of heaven, prepared as a bride adorned for her husband. And I heard a great voice out of heaven saying, Behold, the tabernacle of God is with men, and he will dwell with them, and they shall be his people, and God himself shall be with them, and be their God." Revelation 21:1-3, KJV.

Think of it! A city 375 miles on a side—with its gates and its walls and its foundations—moving steadily and swiftly through space—from heaven to earth!

What a landing strip it will need! But the Saviour himself will prepare it. "And his feet shall stand in that day upon the Mount of Olives, . . . and the Mount of Olives shall cleave in the midst thereof toward the east and toward the west, and there shall be a very great valley; and half of the mountain shall remove toward the north, and half of it toward the south. . . . And

the Lord my God shall come, and all the saints with thee."
Zechariah 14:4, 5, KJV.

What a city! Covering almost the entire Middle East.

Then will follow the final events in the awful history of rebellion. But out of the ashes of this estranged planet will come a
new earth. And when it is all over, the universe will be clean.
One writer describes it this way:

"There are ever-flowing streams, clear as crystal, and beside
them waving trees cast their shadows upon the paths prepared
for the ransomed of the Lord. There the wide-spreading plains
swell into hills of beauty, and the mountains of God rear their
lofty summits. On those peaceful plains, beside those living
streams, God's people, so long pilgrims and wanderers, shall
find a home. . . .

"All the treasures of the universe will be open to the study of
God's redeemed. Unfettered by mortality, they wing their tire-
less flight to worlds afar—worlds that thrilled with sorrow at
the spectacle of human woe and rang with songs of gladness at
the tidings of a ransomed soul. . . . With undimmed vision they
gaze upon the glory of creation—suns and stars and systems,
all in their appointed order circling the throne of Deity. Upon
all things, from the least to the greatest, the Creator's name is
written, and in all are the riches of His power displayed. . . .

"The great controversy is ended. Sin and sinners are no more.
The entire universe is clean. One pulse of harmony and
gladness beats through the vast creation. From Him who created all, flow life and light and gladness, throughout the
realms of illimitable space. From the minutest atom to the
greatest world, all things, animate and inanimate, in their
unshadowed beauty and perfect joy, declare that God is love."
—The Great Controversy, pages 675, 677, 678.

Satisfying picture! The universe is clean. And God's plan, so
long interrupted, at last is carried out. Let me illustrate.

In America's early days, we are told, a family lived in their
wilderness home on the bleak New England shore. It was a
home of their own making, with furniture carved out by their
own hands. There were two grown children. One of them was a
young doctor who was almost constantly away from home, vis-

iting the little towns and isolated settlements along the coast. The other was a lovely girl about twenty.

Each evening she would steal away in the quiet of the nearby wooded sections, without the family's knowing just where she went, to have her quiet devotions alone in nature's retreat. Always she would sing:

> "When softly falls the twilight hour,
> O'er moor and mountain, field and flow'r,
> How sweet to leave a world of care,
> And lift to heav'n the voice of pray'r."

One evening as she enjoyed her meditation, and just as she had completed the first two lines of her little song,

> "When softly falls the twilight hour,
> O'er moor and mountain, field and flow'r,"

a stranger crept up behind her, struck her on the head, and fled. She dropped to the ground, unconscious. Naturally, when the evening meal was served, the girl was missing. A party went out to search for her. She was found, but remained unconscious for several days. The doctor brother was called, and an operation was planned to remove the pressure on the brain.

When it was completed and she had regained consciousness, what do you suppose she did? Her lips began to move, and she finished the song so abruptly interrupted a few days before:

> "How sweet to leave a world of care,
> And lift to heav'n the voice of pray'r."

Her brain began to function just where it had left off.

Just so, God's plan was interrupted—rudely interrupted. It was delayed, but not changed. The song begun in Eden will again be taken up and finished when the earth is restored to its original beauty and man to his original happiness.

The first three chapters of the Bible describe God's original plan, and sin's rude interruption. The last three chapters of the

Bible describe God's plan restored, the music continued. And all the rest of the Bible in between unfolds His program to bring man back to the happiness intended for him.

Remember, "The meek shall inherit the earth." And "If ye be Christ's, then are ye . . . heirs." It is just as simple as that!

And it will all be real. I hope if you get anything out of these words, it will be the conviction that the home of the saved, the future life, will be real. God is real. Christ is real. You will be real.

Our friends will be real. We will recognize each other. How could it be otherwise? The lovable little personality traits which make for happiness here will certainly not be lost.

You remember how Mary stood in the garden, blinded by tears, on the morning of the resurrection. Through her tears she could not recognize her Saviour. She did not expect to see Him alive. She thought Him to be the gardener.

But Jesus quietly spoke just one word—"Mary!" And the characteristic way in which He said her name was unmistakable. Instantly she responded, "Master!"

The resurrection will bring changes, to be sure. But they will be changes for the better. God will take our poor, worn out, imperfect bodies and make them perfect, immortal. Tired, broken, aging bodies—all will be changed. Wonderful news!

Would you like to read the description that God gives of the new earth? Would you like to see how real and practical and satisfying it will be?

"For, behold, I create a new heaven and a new earth: and the former shall not be remembered, nor come into mind." "And they shall build houses, and inhabit them; and they shall plant vineyards, and eat the fruit of them. They shall not build, and another inhabit; they shall not plant, and another eat." Isaiah 65:17, 21, 22, KJV.

Evidently it will be an own-your-own-home proposition. And think how satisfying it all will be. Today we build a lovely home for our comfort and the happiness of our family. We landscape the grounds, and it is not long until the home has the touch of our personality and love. Yet all too soon we die, or the home is left to others.

How wonderfully different it will be in the new earth. For there we shall never die. In that perfect world we shall not build and another inhabit.

And did you know that there is to be health insurance as well? "And the inhabitant shall not say, I am sick: the people that dwell therein shall be forgiven their iniquity." Isaiah 33:24, KJV.

Often the heart chokes with sadness, and even fear, when a little child says to his parent, "I am sick," or when a husband or a wife says, "I am sick." But here will be the finest health insurance of all—perfect bodies with youthful vigor that will never diminish. "They shall run, and not be weary; and they shall walk, and not faint." Isaiah 40:31, KJV.

Sound appealing? No hospitals, for there will be no sick. No psychiatrists, for none will suffer with a guilt complex. All their sins will be forgiven. And there will be no fatigue.

Friend, I can hardly wait. Can you? Imagination ever so wild could not begin to picture the joys and the wonders of God's glorious new world. No wonder the apostle Paul said, "Eye hath not seen, nor ear heard, neither have entered into the heart of man, the things which God hath prepared for them that love him." 1 Corinthians 2:9, KJV.

But best of all, Jesus will be there! Just think of taking hold of a hand and finding it God's hand—the Saviour's hand! What would you give for a privilege like that!

Do I hear you ask, "How can I be there?"

Your question—and your answer—are found in Psalm 24:3, 4, KJV: "Who shall ascend into the hill of the Lord? or who shall stand in his holy place?" And back comes the answer: "He that hath clean hands, and a pure heart."

There is only one way to have clean hands and a pure heart. That is the way of forgiveness through a dying Christ—and the way of a new heart and power to live through a living Christ.

It is the living Christ, the King of glory, who one day soon will lead His people through the gates into their eternal happiness.

And it will be your privilege and mine to participate in that grand event. You need not miss it. A reservation is all you need—your name with the word *pardon* written beside it.

The Godfather's Revenge

It happened one evening in a peaceful village near Palermo, Sicily. Pietro Buscetta parked his little Fiat and stepped into the warm Mediterranean breeze. As he crossed the quiet street to his home, a man jumped out of the shadows. Three shots rang out. Buscetta fell dead, an apparent victim of the Mafia.

Why would the mob want to murder Buscetta? Pietro was a gentle businessman, loved by everyone. Harmless and peaceable, he even pasted the decal "God protects me" on his windshield.

It appeared to be a case of revenge. Pietro was related to Tommaso Buscetta, a reformed Mafia leader whose stunning confession cracked their code of silence. Tommaso's testimony had darkened 3,000 pages with incriminating information, leading to an arrest warrant for 366 Mafiosi. Among those imprisoned were chief bosses, known as godfathers. It was one of the largest crackdowns in the Mafia's long and bloody history.

And the mob was mad about it. Their wrath against Buscetta's relatives was ruthless and relentless. According to *Life* magazine, he lost six members of his family to the revenge of the godfathers.

How did the Mafia become the powerful organization so many fear today? Its roots go back a century and a half to the island of Sicily, south of the mainland of Italy. Beginning as a secret brotherhood controlling orchards and slaughterhouses, it gradually grew stronger and more menacing.

In 1901 the Mafia was exported to the United States. Godfather Don Vito Casioferro, accused of butchering a fellow Italian, escaped to America. Soon he involved himself in organized crime, helping connect the notorious Black Hand gangs of New York City to the Sicilian Mafia.

In 1931, four gangsters hired by Lucky Luciano shot their way through a Park Avenue suite and murdered chief godfather Salvatore Maranzano. Within hours, forty of the old guard were executed, and Luciano reigned as undisputed king of the underworld, ruling over twenty-four family bosses. New York, with five Mafia families, became the stronghold of the mob.

For the next fifty years these five New York families survived and thrived in mystery and secrecy. Occasionally the ruthless rivalry within the brotherhood erupted into public notice, as in the 1979 murder of godfather Carmine Galante. Yet even though the Mafia fought among themselves, they always maintained a united front against the FBI.

Until Tommaso Buscetta broke ranks, never had the mob lost a top-level leader. Buscetta was known as "boss of two worlds" for his operations in Italy and Brazil. His defection inspired thirty other Mafiosi to break their code of silence. Based on their leads, law-enforcement officials taped 4,000 hours of testimony from 171 bugs and wiretaps. A spine-chilling story emerged of bloody extortion, drug-dealing, and prostitution.

Now the FBI had their chance to move in on the mob. Staging a lightning-swift operation, agents captured nine bosses, including all five New York godfathers.

Meanwhile, police held informer Buscetta under tight security in a New Jersey jail. As this is written, he has so far survived the revenge of the godfathers. But sooner or later, they will probably get their man. They usually do.

How would you like to be the target of a godfather's revenge? Well, you are. The Bible says so.

The devil, you see, is identified in Scripture as the god of this world. And Jesus told His enemies that their father was the devil. So Satan is the original godfather of sin on this planet. He is out to get you. We read it in Revelation 12:12, NKJV:

"Rejoice, O heavens, and you who dwell in them! Woe to the inhabitants of the earth and the sea! For the devil has come down to you, having great wrath, because he knows that he has a short time."

What is the story behind this cosmic drama? The Lord Jesus Christ defeated the devil on the cross, exposing the godfather of evil before the onlooking universe. Heaven rejoices because Satan's cruel rule is doomed for an early demise. And the devil is quite angry about it.

But why should Satan vent his wrath upon you and me? It is revenge against God. We are our heavenly Father's children, you see. The devil wants to strike back at God by hurting us. Just as Mafia godfathers take revenge upon those who expose them, by harming their families, so the devil is out to avenge himself upon Christ by attacking His family on earth.

And he has helpers to harass us. He heads a sinister organization even more secretive than the Mafia. Here is how the apostle Paul describes the threat of our enemy:

"We do not wrestle against flesh and blood, but against principalities, against powers, against the rulers of the darkness of this age, against spiritual hosts of wickedness in the heavenly places." Ephesians 6:12, NKJV.

This is serious. The godfather's network of hyperactive demons is determined to abuse you. To confuse you. To torture you with guilt, pain, sorrow, and death.

How can we defend ourselves? Tommaso Buscetta gets round-the-clock protection from the police. Suppose we hire an armed guard. Would that help us defend ourselves against the devil?

No, our foe and his confederates are invisible. How can we confront an enemy we cannot even see? Besides, they are much too cunning and powerful for us to fight.

Are we left helpless? Thank God, no! We have all the shelter we need in the Lord Jesus Christ! Here is what we can do to receive His help: "Put on the whole armor of God, that you may be able to stand against the wiles of the devil." Ephesians 6:11, NKJV.

Just how do we put on God's armor? The same way Jesus did when He walked this earth. He suffered more attacks than we will ever know. How did He survive? "Now in the morning, having risen a long while before daylight, He went out and departed to a solitary place; and there He prayed." Mark 1:35, NKJV.

There we have it! Prayer brings protection.

But we do not pray very much. Oh, we believe in prayer. We talk about it, sing about it—even want laws to enforce prayer in our schools. Then why do we not take time for personal prayer? Why do we not rise early as Jesus did to gather strength for the battle? Day after day we stumble out the door without making contact with God. We fail to feel our need of constant communication with heaven.

An old sailor was spinning one of his hair-raising yarns about his adventures at sea. His eight-year-old grandson listened breathlessly.

"Then the ship lurched against the rock. We heard the terrifying sound of splintering wood. Then the water flooded in as the side gave way."

The wide-eyed little fellow gasped, "What did you do, Grandpa?"

"Well, my boy, all that was left was to pray."

"Oh, no! You mean it was *that bad*?"

It seems that prayer has become our last resort. It is OK for sinking sailors and damsels in distress. Prayer is our fire extinguisher, good only for emergencies.

But how we suffer because we do not take time every day to pray. As the old hymn goes, "O what peace we often forfeit, / O what needless pain we bear, / All because we do not carry / Everything to God in prayer." We are just too busy, running around and around until we get dizzy.

The Reformer Martin Luther accomplished an astonishing amount of good in his life. Five hundred years later we are still reaping the fruit of his labors. What was Luther's secret of success? He took time to pray. In fact, one particularly hectic day he exclaimed, "I have so much to do today that I must spend the first several hours in prayer."

Evidently Martin Luther considered prayer to be good time management. Did he know something we have forgotten? Can prayer actually help us save time? Let us consider several principles of time-efficiency recognized by the business world.

One foundation of time management is setting goals and priorities. Experts tell us to decide what is most important and to stick with it. But it is so easy to become distracted.

Like the farmer who rose early to plow his "south forty." First he needed to oil the old tractor, but he ran out of oil, so he went to the shop to fetch some more. On the way he noticed that the pigs were not fed. He turned aside to the corncrib, where he found some sacks. That reminded him that the potatoes were sprouting, so he started for the potato pit. Passing the woodpile, he remembered that his wife wanted fuel for the stove. As he bent down for some sticks, an ailing chicken limped by. He dropped the wood and reached for the sick bird. When evening came, the poor fellow still had not gotten his tractor to the field.

Obviously, being busy is not enough. We must organize our lives according to what is important, or we risk running around all day accomplishing nothing. Nothing that really matters.

How do we know what is most important? Step back and survey the big picture. What means the most to you? What will last in the long-run?

Most of us live outside our own values. Every survey I have seen reports that health and family are more important to us than wealth or career. Yet we bury ourselves in our work, ignoring our health and our families. Those few who manage to make it to the top often ruin themselves getting there.

Prayer prevents us from ignoring what is precious to us. Communication with God keeps us focused on our priorities. Putting first things first with God every morning helps us stay on track all day long.

What is most important to you? Have you become sidetracked? Pollsters tell us that Americans rank spiritual values high in their priorities. Yet somehow God gets buried amid the rat race. Is this true with you? Jesus wants us to think it through: "What good will it be for a man if he gains the whole world, yet forfeits his soul? Or what can a man give in exchange for his soul?" Matthew 16:26, NIV.

Dennis Barnhart was young and successful. Through his skillful management as president, the Eagle Computer Corporation had doubled its sales every quarter. The day of the first public stock offering, his personal holdings in the company were valued at nine million dollars.

But hours later that same California spring day, a tragic accident ended everything. His red Ferrari swerved out of control, tore through a guard rail, and crashed into a ravine. All of a sudden it did not matter about the business. Or about the red Ferrari. The only thing that mattered was eternity.

Believe me, friend, it is worth the time it takes to keep close to God in prayer.

Another principle of time management is to work with energy and enthusiasm. When we are burdened with bad news, it is hard to get down to business. We cannot accomplish much when we are worried. Or resentful. Or guilty. Or discouraged. Any of this can paralyze our energy, leaving us unable to function well.

In prayer we lay our burdens to rest, exchanging them for peace. After working everything out with the Lord, we feel refreshed. Relieved. Rejuvenated. With God at our side we can do our work with renewed gusto. We accomplish more in less time through Christ, who gives us strength.

It has been the strength of God received in prayer that has kept our nation going in its darkest hours. George Washington nearly surrendered to despair at Valley Forge during the winter of 1777/78. His army wallowed in misery. Lacking training and equipment, one third of the soldiers were unfit to fight. A trail of blood followed their bare feet as they staggered through the snow.

Supplies were short. Farmers sold food, which should have fed the cause of freedom, to the enemy for hard cash, while Washington's warriors weakened from hunger. Then smallpox ravaged their ranks. One fourth of those poor patriots perished. Disheartened, many of the shivering and starving survivors threatened to desert their cause.

Meanwhile, the enemy waited out the winter in the warmth of Philadelphia's cozy fireplaces, planning a spring attack to silence forever the rebellious bell of liberty. The Declaration of Independence seemed doomed for death, along with its struggling supporters. From a human point of view, only a fool had hope.

But they did have prayer. While winter's chilly wind whistled doubt and despair, General Washington knelt on the frozen floor of his tent and poured out his heart to a Higher Power. Because the Father of our Nation took time to pray, he received the energy and enthusiasm he needed to lead our land into freedom. Prayer did not waste his time.

Abraham Lincoln rose from his knees each day to guide our nation through its greatest crisis. You know, if presidents can find the time to pray, the rest of us should too. We need energy just as they do so we can accomplish our tasks.

One more key in time management is working with others to get things done. Hostile relationships waste time. They spark political conflicts at the office. Lawsuits against neighbors. Misunderstandings with in-laws. Battles with loved ones at home. How much time we waste at war!

Prayer brings peace. When we pray, God smooths our relationships. Hearts melt. Enemies become friends.

Chuck Colson, who served time for his role in the Watergate affair, often returns behind bars to visit inmates. Recently he brought a witnessing team to the Indiana State Prison. They rubbed shoulders with criminals so vicious that society declared they must die. Yet here they were, gentle as lambs, arms linked in prayer with their visitors.

One of the prisoners invited a team member into his cell to kneel with him in prayer. When they parted, Colson remarked, "You seemed to know that man. Had you met before?"

"Yes," he responded. "I'm Judge Clements—the one who sentenced him to death. I seldom saw anyone so hostile and insensitive as that fellow during his trial. Since I represented society, I was his enemy. But today he's my brother. We feel as close as members of the same family."

Friend, if prayer can achieve a reconciliation like that, it can iron out your daily relationships too. It is hardly what you would call a waste of time!

I hope you can see why prayer is good time management. Yet perhaps you have been praying more but enjoying it less. What is the secret of a satisfying prayer relationship? Do we need a fancy vocabulary to impress the Lord? Maybe a good prayer book?

I have one bit of advice. Relax. Keep your prayers simple. Remember that you are talking with a friend. Just open up your heart to God. Tell Him everything on your mind.

You may wonder how long your prayers should be. That reminds me of the question they asked Abe Lincoln: "How long should a man's legs be?" You know his answer—"A man's legs should be long enough to reach the ground."

Well, that's about how long our prayers should be. They should be long enough to get to the bottom of things with the Lord. Some days you will need more time with Him than on other days. Just make sure you stay with Him long enough to satisfy your soul.

Jesus said we must become as little children. You know how they are—simple, trusting, affectionate, honest.

Of course, children do not always set a good example. I think of the little girl who prayed,"Lord, please make Boston the capital of Vermont, because I said so on my test paper."

Some things, like the capital of Vermont, will probably never be changed. Not even through prayer. In our limited wisdom, we do not know what needs changing and what does not. So when we pray, we trust the results to God. Because Father knows best.

I wonder if you have heard the parable of the three trees that lived in the forest long ago. John Ellis Large tells it in his book *Think on These Things:*

"The first tree prayed that, when it was hewn down, it might become part of the timbers of a noble palace, the most magnificent building ever shaped by the creative hands of men. . . . Instead, it was faced with the bitter fact that its lovely grain was being used to throw a rude stable together. But it was the stable in which the Christ Child was born!

"The second tree petitioned God that, when the ax should be laid to its roots, its planks might be fashioned into the hull of the lordliest vessel that ever sailed the seven seas. . . . Instead, when it was chopped down, it was used to form the hull of a lowly fishing vessel; and the tree resented the insult to its grandeur. But that insignificant schooner was the one from which Jesus preached His incomparable words at the edge of the little Sea of Galilee!

"The third tree beseeched God that it might never feel the bite of the cruel ax, but that it might go on for years pointing its proud finger toward the sky. . . . Instead, the dark day came when the woodsmen arrived and laid the sharp blade to its resisting roots; and it cried out against God with every blow. But the shaken tree was fated to become the crossarms and the upright of the cross of Calvary, destined to point its noble finger toward the sky forever!

"Not a single one of those trees lived to see its fondest wish come true. Not a single one got its deepest prayer answered, nor its own will fulfilled. But God, in fulfilling His will for those three trees, granted them a fulfillment infinitely beyond anything they could have desired or hoped for!"

You can trust a God like that. He will not only protect you from the godfather's revenge—He will fill your life with joy and peace and purpose. Tell me, friend—is He worth your time in prayer?

The Bounty Bible

The way of a ship at sea! Few understood it better, in their time, than the two young men of our story. It's the talk of a tiny island set like a jewel in the South Pacific. And a Book that rode the waves, silent and forgotten, waiting to be found. And then it changed everything!

Captain William Bligh had risen fast in the British Navy. As a young man he had served, and learned well, under the famed English explorer James Cook. It was Cook who introduced better practices of shipboard hygiene and diet into the Navy. And Bligh was quick to carry out his ideas.

Bligh copied his hero in something else too—his violent temper. Cook was known for his outbursts of temper, for his flogging and his cruelty. Yet he seemed to inspire in his men a loyalty that bordered on worship. Bligh, on the other hand, was lenient, reluctant to flog anyone. Yet his violent and cruel outbursts, his constant belittling of those who served under him, wounded and cut more deeply than Cook's ever did. And of course here, on any long voyage, were the seeds of mutiny.

The other young man was Fletcher Christian—all who recall the historic details of the mutiny on the Bounty remember his name.

Fletcher Christian's background was far different from that of Bligh. The Christian family, unquestionably of Scandinavian origin, can be traced back to the 13th century. They were a privileged family, with members assured at birth of both social standing and fortune.

169

These two men, so different, but bound by a common interest and superior skill in navigation, were to sail together—this time on the HMS *Bounty*. The ship and its crew were commissioned to bring back breadfruit plants from Tahiti.

And so it was that on December 23, 1787, the HMS *Bounty* sailed into history, never to return!

Fletcher Christian was sailing as master's mate. He was twenty-three at the time.

And somewhere aboard, safe and dry and forgotten, somewhere in Fletcher's possessions, was a book—a Bible given him by his mother. Did he know it was there?

Well, the plan was to head for the tip of South America, go around it, and take the most direct route to Tahiti. But the attempt to sail around the Horn at that time of year was terrifying. And when Bligh saw that his men couldn't take any more, he gave the order to abandon the Horn and head for the Cape of Good Hope at the southern tip of Africa, taking a roundabout but safer route to Tahiti.

Then came Tahiti, with its relaxed lifestyle in which there were almost no rules. The tropical paradise of flowers and women was intoxicating. The trip could wait. Heaven could wait. The men were satisfied with earth.

Tahitian life, however, was not the cause of the horrors to come. Bligh's problems were closer home. He was irritable beyond description. Nothing anyone did was right. Fletcher Christian was now the target of his wrath. As second in command, his authority, of course, was being eroded.

Finally it was back on ship and goodbye to Tahiti. Bligh's harassment of Christian intensified. At one point, Fletcher said to his captain, "Sir, your abuse is so bad that I cannot do my duty with any pleasure. I have been in hell for weeks with you."

Every man has his breaking point. Fletcher had reached his. Later that day, after further abuse from Bligh, the carpenter saw Fletcher run from the quarter deck with great tears in his eyes. It was the first time any of the crew had seen this strong man in tears.

But now, as he wept, he protested, "I would rather die ten thousand deaths than to bear this treatment."

The abuse—the threats—the blackmail. It was all too much. Sanity was fast departing the *Bounty*.

Fletcher would not lower himself to battle with his captain. He wouldn't defy him. Mutiny was far from his mind. Rather, he decided to leave the ship and trust his future to the open sea. He began giving away his curios and collecting a store of food, nails, and other barter items.

At four in the morning, after only an hour of sleep, Fletcher got up to command his watch. A friend, knowing of his plan to leave the ship, urged him again to stay, assuring him that there was tremendous support for him among the men. It was he, not Bligh, to whom the men looked for leadership and sympathy. He told him the men were "ripe for anything." He didn't say, "ripe for mutiny." He didn't have mutiny in mind.

But suddenly, in his friend's words, Fletcher saw an alternate to his plan to escape. After all, why should *he* leave? Why shouldn't the cantankerous Bligh leave? He was the one at fault.

The moment was right. The ship was his for the taking. It took only minutes for friends to round up a group of supporters and place weapons in their hands. Quickly they decided on their plan. There were to be threats, but no bloodshed. The ship would be taken with force, but with little fuss. Fletcher's face turned stern—"darker than thunder," it is said. And from that moment he kept everyone in fear of himself—even his own men.

Slowly, with two others, he climbed down to where the captain lay sleeping. Bursting in, with a flash of steel, he shouted, "Bligh, you are my prisoner!"

The bewildered captain, protested and pleaded and promised, but to no avail. The plan was to force him into the small boat with four other troublesome men. Some others asked permission to go along—not because of personal loyalty to Bligh, but because the risk of sailing into the South Pacific oblivion or being caught and executed by the British Navy, seemed greater than the risks of survival in a small boat. The launch was put over the side. And the still astonished Bligh, with eighteen companions for whom he had often expressed his contempt, was set adrift on the open sea.

The horrors and dangers that lay ahead for these eighteen can scarcely be imagined. But Bligh was a good navigator. And forty-one days later they would reach Timor, more than 1,200 leagues away, without the loss of a man.

Still aboard the *Bounty* were twenty-five men. Fletcher Christian was now fully in charge. But now that the ship was his, what would he do with it?

And remember, somewhere on that ship, still forgotten and undisturbed, was Fletcher Christian's Bible.

And in it God has said through the prophet, Isaiah:

"So shall my words be that goeth forth out of my mouth: it shall not return unto me void, but it shall accomplish that which I please, and it shall prosper in the thing whereto I send it." Isaiah 55:11, KJV.

A staggering promise under circumstances such as these. Did God know what was going on? What good could possibly come from a situation like this? But wait!

As the ship sailed off into the horizon, no one would know its destination or the fate of those aboard for twenty full years.

The mutineers returned to Tahiti where they were welcomed. But Fletcher Christian knew now that an island, to be a suitable and safe home for British Navy mutineers, must be *uninhabited*. They didn't want to be caught and punished. A book in the *Bounty* library described a tiny island called Pitcairn. It was believed to be without human life. It seemed to be the perfect answer, and the *Bounty* set sail for the long voyage.

But Pitcairn was not where it was supposed to be. This encouraged Christian. For the island was said to be isolated by unimaginable stretches of water, and pounded by a violent surf that made landing almost impossible. If it was also mischarted, detection would be very, very difficult. If Fletcher could only find it, it would be like sailing a ship himself and his cargo of human beings straight off the face of the earth into oblivion, so he thought.

He zigzagged along the line of latitude until at last, on the fifteenth day of January, Pitcairn loomed ahead: a giant, lonely rock, less than two square miles, lifting itself high out of the sea. But even then the *Bounty* must wait, tortured by a violent swell, for forty-eight hours before a landing could be attempted.

Pitcairn was all it was said to be—and more.

Isolated. Difficult of access. No sign of human life. Its flat summit invisible from the sea. Plenty of water. Vegetables growing wild. Coconut trees. Candle-nut trees for light. Mulberry trees for making cloth. No mosquitos.

With wife and friends and freedom, who could ask for more? It was a veritable Garden of Eden.

The early days were difficult but happy as all worked together to remove from the ship everything that could be moved. The mast and spars of a square-rigger could so easily betray their presence to any passing ship. Yet they dared not dismantle the boat too soon. For what if there *was* human life on the island—still in hiding?

Then, less than two weeks after their arrival, the *Bounty* was ablaze. No one knows who set it burning. The die was cast. Their only means of escape was devoured before their eyes!

When at last, in 1808, two ships did stop at Pitcairn, they found only one surviving mutineer. He was John Adams. He was the only adult male on the island along with four Tahitian women—women who had been taken with them from Tahiti. The rest were children and teenagers.

But one thing was evident in those encounters with passing ships. Something had happened to the community. Something very good. Something awesome. Something having to do with Fletcher Christian's Bible.

Glynn Christian of London, England, ever since he learned at the age of nine that he is a descendant of the original *Bounty,* has been fired with the desire to know everything there is to know about Fletcher Christian, his ancestor. What was he like? What was his family like? What was the mutiny all about? What finally happened to him? He has spent years in careful research, even to spending considerable time on Pitcairn himself.

Out of it all he has written a remarkable and highly interesting book—*Fragile Paradise*. He has tried to be objective, to be fair, to present all of the conflicting accounts. Much of the information in this chapter has come from this book. We are indebted to Glynn for this. Thank you again, Glynn Christian!

Briefly, this is what happened. And remember that there are conflicting accounts. If what I say doesn't agree with what you have heard, you will understand.

Evidently, life on Pitcairn *was* sort of paradise for a time. But it was a flawed paradise. No man-made utopia will endure for long while the hearts of men are unchanged.

Fletcher Christian's Bible, if he had read it, would have told him it couldn't last. For we read: "Except the Lord build the house, they labour in vain that build it: except the Lord keep the city, the watchman waketh but in vain." Psalm 127:1, KJV.

No paradise built upon men's passion, and tarnished by their unforgiven guilt, can endure for long.

Evidently the problem of "not enough women for the men" flared up again. The mutineers began killing each other off— until only John Adams was left. Someone even killed Fletcher Christian.

Adams suddenly realized the awful responsibility that was now his. Here were these children, fathered by the mutineers— some of them Fletcher Christian's own children. These children were in his hands. Their future would be the future that he, John Adams, created for them.

It was then that he remembered Fletcher Christian's Bible. It was the only book on the island. But with that book, that Bible, he taught those children how to read and how to write— and how to live. The effect was phenomenal. The children grew up to be well-mannered, orderly, dedicated Christian youth.

It was this unusual interest in the Word of God, and the amazing transformation in the entire population of the island, that attracted the attention first of passing vessels, then of the British Government, and finally of the whole world. For such secrets cannot be kept.

It was interest in this little paradise in the Pacific that led thousands of Christians in North America to gather funds for the purchase of a ship. They equipped it and launched it for the sole purpose of caring for the spiritual and physical needs of people on Pitcairn and other islands of the South Seas.

It was on October 2, 1890, that the *Pitcairn* set sail from San

Francisco harbor. It was just 100 years after another ship, the *Bounty*, had unloaded her last crew and passengers—the escaping mutineers.

The *Pitcairn* was loaded with gifts. There were thousands of dollars worth of Christian books. The crew was made up of sturdy Christian seamen. Its passengers were dedicated missionaries. As it sailed out of the harbor on that initial trip, friends and relatives waved them on their eventful way.

Can you imagine the excitement and joy of the Pitcairn people as they sighted the tiny ship and then learned its mission?

Today Pitcairn is a Seventh-day Adventist island. Life revolves around the church—and the school—the close-knit community—and the sea. Every passing ship is met by the Pitcairners in their longboats loaded with souvenirs. Passengers on the ship are covered with flowers as the longboats pull away and head again for Pitcairn. And floating across the waves is heard the sound of the islanders as they sing for the ship their parting hymn.

But I think again of Fletcher Christian, the original mutineer. High up on Pitcairn is a scoop in the rock called Fletcher Christian's Cave. It is said that Fletcher, usually cheerful and hard-working, would sometimes become depressed and retire to that spot for days.

Think, if you will, what his thoughts must have been as he gazed out over the sea. Try to imagine the torture of not knowing what was happening out there beyond his vision. Was he, in the eyes of the world, only an outlaw, a mutineer? Was he even now being pursued? Did his family know what had really happened? Was anyone telling them the truth? Did the launch set adrift with Captain Bligh ever reach a safe harbor? Or were all lost at sea? And if they were, was he, Fletcher Christian, a murderer too? There is no torture in the world like the torture of guilt!

If only Fletcher Christian had remembered his Bible! He could have read these words:

"Though your sins be as scarlet, they shall be as white as snow; though they be red like crimson, they shall be as wool." Isaiah 1:18, KJV.

But I ask you, How do we know that Fletcher Christian *didn't* remember his Bible? How do we know that he *didn't* find in it a Saviour and forgiveness for his guilt?

I want to read you a very precious verse of Scripture: "The Lord shall count, when he writeth up the people, that this man was born there." Psalm 87:6, KJV.

God does not excuse sin. But He forgives it. And He takes into account where a man is born. He knows the tragic circumstances in which he has been trapped. He knows how much the human mind can take before it snaps.

Could it be that the story of Flecther Christian is not over yet? Jesus is coming soon. When He sends His angels to gather His people, lonely Pitcairn will not be forgotten. And could it be that Fletcher Christian—mutineer forgiven—will be among those the Lord Jesus counts as His own? I hope so!

If other Fletcher Christians, by whatever name, are reading these words now—men with a lonely guilt like his—they too can be forgiven. You, too, can be forgiven—just now.

What Is God Like?

All of us have wondered about the one who stands at the helm of the cosmic ship. The One who made the worlds—and holds the stars in their orbits—and knows when even a sparrow falls.

What is God like? Can we know? Can anybody know? Or is God a tightly-locked mystery you aren't supposed to understand? How can you worship—and love—and trust—a mystery—a Stranger you don't know? Is that your dilemma?

A lot of ideas about God are being dispensed. Some are fact. And some are propaganda. Is it possible that you haven't been told the truth about God?

Maybe you ought to know!

Have you ever noticed how quickly the problems of life are whittled down to size when you look up at the stars on a clear night?

Harry Golden wrote a little piece that he calls, "Why I Never Bawl Out a Waitress." He says, "I have a rule against registering complaints in a restaurant."

Why? Because he knows "that there are at least four billion suns in the Milky Way—which is only one galaxy." He goes on to describe the incalculable numbers, the incredible speeds, the incomprehensible distances in the cosmic parade that revolves over our heads. Then he remembers that even "within the range of our biggest telescopes there are at least one hundred million separate galaxies such as our own Milky Way, and . . . that the further you go out into space with the telescopes the thicker the galaxies become."

177

So he concludes, "When you think of all this, it's silly to worry about whether the waitress brought you string beans instead of limas!"

Yes, the night sky can make our problems seem pretty trivial. And us too!

But what about the God who is out there guiding all those stars? What is He like? Does He know we're here? Does He care what happens to us? What is He thinking when He looks down from the top side of the sky?

However we may word it, however we may express it, however we may try to cover it up—that's the big question in all our minds. What is God like? How does He feel toward this spinning, sinning planet?

Tom Braden, in his delightful book *Eight Is Enough,* tells of the time he became so frustrated with his family of unpredictable teenagers that he just resigned from being father. Temporarily, of course.

But does God ever feel like that? Does He get so tired of our dullness, so weary of our rebellion, so frustrated with our foolish escapades that He feels like resigning His job? What if He should walk out on us one of these days and leave us to spin ourselves into oblivion? What if He already has?

We need to know. Because how can we trust a God we don't know—a God who is a Stranger to us? How can we face the future with any peace of mind at all?

Surprising as it may seem, we read in the book of Job, probably the first book of the Bible ever written, "Acquaint now thyself with him, and be at peace." Job 22:21, KJV.

What do you think of that? The way to find peace of mind is to get acquainted with God—to know what He is like!

Millions today are searching desperately for peace of mind. They are turning to astrology, to Eastern religions—anywhere, everywhere. But evidently if they would just get acquainted with God they could call off their search!

But you say, "Pastor Vandeman, I thought we weren't supposed to understand God. Doesn't the Bible say that the secret things belong to Him?"

Yes, it does. But let's read that scripture, because it says more. "The secret things belong unto the Lord your God: but those things which are revealed belong unto us and to our children." Deuteronomy 29:29, KJV.

Some things about God are kept secret. They aren't for us to understand. But many things about God are revealed. Is it possible that we just haven't bothered with the things that are revealed—with the things that tell us what God is like? Have we thrown out the revelation with the mystery?

It's true that much about God is a mystery. But would He be God if we could bring Him down to our level, if we could fit Him into our little box of brains?

If you can read a physics book and understand everything in it, then it's reasonable to conclude that your understanding of the subject is on a par with that of the physicist who wrote it. Right?

If we could understand all about God, if we could understand everything in the Bible, if our minds could grasp it all, then how would God be superior to us? Do we want a God no bigger than we? Could we trust a God no wiser than we?

Isn't it a little ridiculous for minds that God created to put Him on trial and reject Him because we can't understand all about Him?

Listen. We see the fire in the thundercloud. We call it electricity. We don't understand it. We don't understand how the clouds get their charge. We don't even understand the hatching of a robin's egg. Then should it be any surprise that much about God is a mystery?

Should it be any surprise that we can't understand how God could have already existed—how God could be three Persons and yet one Person—or how the Son of God could come down to earth and be born of a virgin?

Love and faith are at home with mystery. And reason doesn't have to resign its job. It can kneel in reverence before that which it doesn't understand.

We need to get off our stolen thrones and stop trying to bring God down to a level where we can manage Him. We need to stop worrying about the mystery and find peace of mind in what the Bible has revealed about God!

Unfortunately, what God has told us about Himself has been clouded and confused by stuffy theological terms that frighten us away, words like *omnipotent* and *omniscient* and *omnipresent* and *immutable*.

But do you know something? Those words aren't meant to scare us. Those words, if we would just translate them into simple words we can understand, would give us tremendous peace of mind!

For instance, there's the word *omnipotent*. This just means that God is all-powerful. He has all power. There isn't any power, any degree of power, that He doesn't have.

God said it still more simply when He said to Jeremiah, "I am the Lord, the God of all flesh: is there any thing too hard for me?" Jeremiah 32:27, KJV.

Nothing is too hard for God. Don't you like that? Doesn't it give you peace of mind to know that God won't meet up with anything He can't handle—in the universe or in your personal life? If He could create the world, He ought to be able to handle anything that might come up in your life or mine—don't you think?

We are told that God is *omniscient*. But don't let that frighten you. It just means that God is all-knowing. He knows everything—even knows it ahead of time. He says, "I am God, and there is none like me, declaring the end from the beginning, and from ancient times the things that are not yet done." Isaiah 46:9, 10, KJV.

Doesn't that give you peace of mind? Doesn't that give you confidence? God knows all about the future. And if there's anything in the future that we need to know, He'll tell us. Said the prophet Amos, "Surely the Lord God will do nothing, but he revealeth his secret unto his servants the prophets." Amos 3:7, KJV.

And why does He tell the prophets? So they can tell us.

Well, there's the *immutability* of God. That means that God does not change. He is always the same. He cannot change for the better, because He is already perfectly holy, perfectly just, perfectly good. And He cannot change for the worse, because if He did He would no longer be God. He says, "I am the Lord, I change not." Malachi 3:6, KJV.

And we read, "Jesus Christ the same yesterday, and today, and forever." Hebrews 13:8, KJV.

Isn't that wonderful? Did you ever dream what was locked up in some of those big words? God never changes. We don't have to worry about what He'll be like tomorrow!

We say that God is *omnipresent*. And that, of course, means that God, by His Spirit, can be everywhere at once. Jesus said, "I am with you alway, even until the end of the world." Matthew 28:20, KJV.

Don't you like that? Never alone. God right at our side when we need Him. We don't have to be put on a waiting list. We aren't put off because He's out taking care of a galaxy somewhere. We don't rush to our knees in some emergency only to find that He has 17,000 people ahead of us. He's always with us, giving His full attention to us, as if *we* were the only *person* in existence!

You can't understand it? Neither can I. But thank God for it!

And now we come to what appears to be the simplest statement of all about God. The apostle John says it in three short words: "God is love." 1 John 4:8, KJV.

Simplest of all? No. Most complex of all. Hardest of all to understand!

John didn't say, *God is loving*. Lots of people are loving—sometimes. He didn't say, *God exercises love*. Lots of people do that—sometimes. He said, God *is* love. Love in the absolute. So loving it would be impossible to be more loving. There's nobody else like that!

Have you noticed that every one of these attributes of God, these characteristics of God, have been in the absolute? Absolute power. Absolute wisdom. Absolute love. So powerful it would be impossible to have more power. So wise it would be impossible to be wiser. So loving it would be impossible to be more loving!

Do you see what that means? If He has absolute power and absolute wisdom and absolute love, then we have absolute safety in trusting Him. The apostle Paul says, "We know that all things work together for good to them that love God." Romans 8:28, KJV.

What do we have to fear? However God may lead us, however mysterious it may seem at the moment, however difficult it may be to understand, we can have perfect confidence in His leading. God never makes a mistake. If whatever He does for us is the most loving thing possible, what more could we ask?

Think of it this way. Because God is all-loving, He *wants* us to have the best. Because He is all-wise, He *knows* what is best. And because He is all-powerful, He is *able* to carry it out!

God *is* love. It will take all eternity to understand a God like that. But it takes only a moment to trust Him. It takes only a moment to discover the peace of mind that comes with even beginning to know Him!

You see, God had a problem. Man, by his rebellion, had separated himself from God. The happy relationship was broken. God wanted to restore it. Century after century He tried. But how could men understand what God was like? Words and messages by means of prophets and angels were not enough. And so God sent Jesus to show what God is like.

That's why He came. See Him walking through village after village, healing all their sick. Hear Him saying to the woman whose accusers had dragged her into His presence, "Neither do I condemn you. Go, and sin no more." Watch Him making a long trip because He knew that a woman of a foreign nation wanted her daughter healed. See Him feeding the people when they were hungry. Marvel at His patience with men who all wanted to be the greatest. Stand back amazed as you see Him washing the feet of the one who would betray Him!

See Him praying in the garden, crushed by the weight of a world's guilt. See Him tempted to call legions of angels to bear Him away from a hostile planet. See Him fiercely tempted to come down from the cross and show everybody who He was. But see Him staying there to the very end, till His work was finished, because He remembered you—and me. That's what God is like!

But God has a problem—still. He has an enemy who is spreading false propaganda, telling lies about His character. And that enemy has been desperately successful. He got the people of Christ's day so hopelessly mixed up that they rejected their Saviour. The men who were supposed to know God best, were the ones who knew Him least. They understood God's justice—but they knew nothing of His mercy. And so they crucified the One who had come to save them!

You remember the story Jesus told—about the man who sowed wheat in his field and then weeds came up with the wheat? His helpers asked him where the weeds came from, and He said, "An enemy has done this."

So when you see the weeds, when you see the plane crashes and the floods and the fires and the hurricanes and innocent children dying of leukemia and all the rest—remember that an enemy is responsible. Not God. It's Satan, the enemy, who plots all the heartache and destruction—and then blames it on God.

No. The One who cares is the One who died there without protest. It's God dying to save guilty man. It's God trying to save the ones who put Him there, trying to save the ones who drove the nails. It's God dying in your place. In my place. That's what God is like? He's the one who cares!

And listen. The suffering of God didn't begin or end at the cross. Ever since man chose to go his own way, God has felt the hurt. He feels the loneliness and the estrangement more deeply than we. Because He loves as never man has loved, because His love is absolute, He feels the hurt far more deeply than we ever could!

We think selfishly of a day when all heartache will be over. But what about God? He's hurting more than we. He longs for that day more than we!

But you say, "If God is all-powerful, why doesn't He do something? Why doesn't He put a stop to it all?"

He will, friend. He will. Just as soon as we've seen enough of sin. Just as soon as we've understood enough how deadly it is. Just as soon as we've grown tired enough of this rebel planet. When we're so fed up with sin, so disgusted with it, when we hate it so much that we'll never sin again—then God can trust us with a life that never ends. Then He can know—and we can know—and all the universe can know—that it will never happen again!

In the meantime, just a little longer, God permits the suffering to continue. He sends warnings. He sends the little judgments—so we'll avoid the big judgments soon to come. He calls us away from danger, away from the precipice, away from certain death—and weeps His heart out when we don't come. That's what God is like!

Friend, do you understand just a little more what God is like? No other knowledge is so important. No other knowledge brings such peace of mind!

A teacher, at the end of the year, in the final examination, made this the final question: "What one thing have you learned this year that will be with you five years from now?"

One young student answered that question with one word: "You."

One day soon we'll all face the final examination. And if God should ask us, "What one thing have you learned that will stay with you forever?"—I hope that every one of us may answer, "You, Lord!"

God's High Country

It was in January of the year 1844 that John Charles Fremont reduced an aged Indian to tears by asking him a question.
How could a man cross the mountains at some of the gentler
elevations southwest of Lake Tahoe?

The Indian replied that the trail was very hard. It would take
six sleeps in summer. And in winter a man should not go at all.
"Rock on rock, snow on snow," he chanted. "And even if you get
over the snow you will not be able to get down from the mountain."

Fremont went anyway!

The Indians were sensible about such things. They knew a
barrier when they saw one. They didn't have to climb a mountain just because it was there. Their curiosity about what was
on the other side didn't cancel out their good sense. If a range of
mountains was in the way, they just didn't bother about what it
might be hiding!

Of course, this was not an ordinary mountain range. These
were not ordinary mountains. When the Spanish missionary,
Fray Pedro Font, first saw these gleaming peaks from the west,
two hundred years ago, he named then *una gran sierra
nevada*—a great snowy range!

And so it is. For the Sierra splits the state of California for
400 miles—from just below Mount Lassen in the north until it
peters out into cactus flats near the town of Mojave in the
south.

The High Sierra is undoubtedly the most dramatic stretch of

wilderness in the old continental United States. Wherever you look, the eye is overwhelmed by the immensity of rock, by the presence of rock, by the power of rock. Rock so formidable it boggles the mind. Rock in the sheerest of cliffs. Rock heaved and tossed in beautiful disarray into the deepest of canyons. Rock that rises in terrible sawteeth to the summit of 14,494-foot Mount Whitney—the tallest mountain in the old forty-eight states. Its wall stands two full miles above the valley floor!

And talk about waterfalls! The Yosemite tumbles and free-falls 2,565 feet into the Merced River. And in case you don't remember—the famed Niagara is only 167 feet!

Nowhere is there a more beautiful valley than Yosemite. It seems not to belong in this world. No one who has ever seen its white granite walls gleaming in the moonlight will ever forget the sight. Those walls of monolithic rock rise on either side from 3,000 to 4,800 feet above the valley floor—El Capitan, Half Dome, Sentinel Rock, Glacier Point. It was from Glacier Point that for many years fire was pushed over the edge at nine o'clock each summer evening—to cascade down the sheer wall in the famous firefall of Yosemite!

With all the formidable geology of the High Sierra, it is no wonder that the Indians hesitated to cross it!

Mark Twain roughed it through the Sierra. He wrote, "The air up there . . . is very pure and fine, bracing and delicious. And why shouldn't it be? It is the same the angels breathe!"

And of course there was John Muir. He belonged to the Sierra, as the Sierra belonged to him. The high country, to him, was a passion. He said, "Climb the mountains and get their good tidings. Nature's peace will flow into you as sunshine flows into trees. The winds will blow their own freshness into you, and the storms their energy, while cares will drop off like autumn leaves."

It is impossible to visit the High Sierra, even for the first time, without the strong, deep feeling that *something has happened here.* Something tremendous, something catastrophic, something beyond the reach of imagination. Said one visitor, as horses were reined beside some rockslides, "See how that granite pushed its way right up there between the volcanic and metamorphic rock? The rock is standing right on end. In fact, this whole country is standing on end!"

What happened—to make the whole country stand on end? What were the forces that created this bold, dramatic, wild, beautifully disordered landscape? You can't look at Half Dome in Yosemite—that 4,800-foot mass of granite whose face is a sheer, perpendicular wall—without wondering how it got that way. Albrecht Penck, a European geologist, when he first saw the 10,895-foot wall of the Mount Whitney scarp, asked to be left alone for a time so that he could contemplate it in silence!

It was not so long ago that a Sequoia National Park ranger strolled into a crowd of about 300 who had made the climb from the Owens Valley to the granite summit of Mount Whitney. One of the hikers, simply awed by the sight of the two-mile plunge down to the valley floor, asked the ranger how the Sierra came to be shaped as it is.

The ranger had had a smattering of geology, and he replied, "Well, this summit plateau is part of the old landscape that was lying here as kind of a rolling lowland millions of years ago. Then the whole Sierra was bowed up like an arch." More people turned to listen, and he went on, "Then the keystone collapsed to form this great escarpment going down into the Owens Valley, with the White Mountains over there to the east making the other half of the broken arch. And later, through erosion and glaciation, we got the final shaping of the land—the meadows and canyons and peaks and bowls—as you see them all around you today."

The ranger paused to let all that information soak in, and one of the hikers spoke up and said, "I don't believe what you're saying. The Bible said the Lord made the world in six days and the flood destroyed God's plan!"

The ranger replied thoughtfully, "Well, yes it does; it says that." And he wandered off by himself to think about it. Months later he hadn't thought of a more suitable reply. "What could I tell the guy?" he shrugged. "Besides, maybe he was right!"

Ezra Bowen, who tells the story, comments, "Maybe he was." He says that "today the most sophisticated earth scientists, not to mention the fundamentalists, are still groping among the particulars of the Sierra's creation."

Believe it or not, I didn't find that story where you might expect—in a book written by a creationist. I found it, of all places, in a Time-Life book *The High Sierra!*

It may be that even that Sequoia ranger realized that the hiker's explanation—God's explanation—is far less complicated, far more reasonable, far easier to believe than the popular but changing theories of geologists. The Bible says simply, "For in six days the Lord made heaven and earth." Exodus 20:11, KJV.

No fallen arches. No collapsing keystones. No long periods of time. Just six days. And it was done. Said David, "By the word of the Lord the heavens were made, and by the breath of his mouth all their host. . . . For he spoke, and it was done; he commanded, and it stood fast." Psalm 33:6-9, NASB.

Think of it! He just spoke. And there it was!

But did God create it like it is now—in all the disorder and desolation and disarray? No. As you see the High Sierra today, you can only conclude that, beautiful and grand as it is, whatever has happened here is something that was never meant to be!

John Muir thought glaciers were responsible. But the cantankerous Josiah Whitney, after whom Mount Whitney was named, said, "No glaciers." And if he said, "No glaciers," that's what you'd better believe. He was very sure of himself. He was especially sure that Yosemite Valley had been created by a monstrous collapse of the earth floor.

Was it? The great earthquake of March 1872 gave us some indication of the awesome force it would take to create Yosemite Valley. For several hours severe tremors rumbled through the high country. The Owens Valley was split in a way that brought sheer terror to all who lived through it. Of course not many people were living anywhere near. That's the only reason there was not a tremendous loss of life.

A forty-acre field sank seven feet. A small lake disappeared. The Owens River ran upstream for a time until its bed was dry. In the darkness, according to one account, "people watched cas-

cades of rock roaring down the mountains in monstrous ava-
lanches, throwing out such brilliant trails of sparks that they
were assumed to be flows of lava."

This was John Muir's "noble earthquake." Yosemite was 120
miles from the epicenter, but still well within the scope of its
convulsions.

There was a tremendous roar as the Eagle Rock on the south
wall gave way. Thousands of great boulders poured to the valley floor in a sort of free curve—friction giving it the appear-
ance of an arc of glowing fire!

The roar of scraping rock was indescribable. Trying to give
some idea of the volume of the awful sound, John Muir said, "It
seems to me that if all the thunder of all the storms I had ever
heard were condensed into one roar it would not equal this
rock-roar!"

This Owens Valley earthquake of 1872 was one of the great
earthquakes of all history. But it brought little change to the
face of the Sierra. Other than the rockslides, the most notice-
able scar on the whole Sierra—after this giant earthquake—
was "one wistful little breastwork threading across three miles
of the Owens Valley floor and rising perhaps twenty-three feet
at the highest point."

Think of it! All this sound and fury, and it left a mark three
miles long and twenty-three feet high. The Sierra scarp loom-
ing over Lone Pine is almost 500 times that high. What would
it have taken to shape the Sierra as we see it today? How many
earthquakes would it take to carve out Yosemite—Half Dome,
El Capitan, and all?

There must be some better answers than those the geologists
have been repeating—most of the geologists, that is. Some are
beginning to wonder. Says Ezra Bowen, "California's earth scientists recently fell to doubting whether there had ever been a
Sierra arch at all, with keystones that collapsed to form the
eastern valley; or whether the whole range had not been built
by some other force not yet fathomed."

What do you think of that? "Some other force not yet
fathomed." But God tells us what that other force was. God tells
us that water did it!

The book of Genesis says, "More and more the waters increased over the earth until they covered all the high mountains everywhere under heaven. The waters increased and the mountains were covered to a depth of fifteen cubits." Genesis 7:19, 20, NEB.

Water enough to cover all the high mountains everywhere. That's a lot of water! And some of you know by experience that water can be very, very violent!

This wasn't a quiet little rainstorm. The water didn't just quietly rise until it covered the mountains. More than water was involved. This was global catastrophe!

The trouble is that there is nothing in our experience that can qualify us to understand the Flood. The entire planet was involved. The earth was torn and twisted and convulsed in a way that our imaginations simply cannot reach.

Start with rain. Add cloudbursts. Add water gushing forth from the earth. Add tidal waves. Add fire. Add wind. Add volcanoes. Add twisting and turning. Add mountains rising and falling. Add the most violent convulsions, the wildest upheavals. Add everything you can think of. And we still cannot begin to appreciate what happened in Noah's day. Not a catastrophe of a moment. Rather, it must have been centuries before the earth quieted down!

Now you know what happened to the High Sierra!

And yet with all the scars of that global catastrophe—along with all the marks that our own grubby fingers have left on the high country—it still hasn't lost its grandeur. God's original creation—even when torn and twisted and heaved and tossed and stood on end—still bears the signature of a loving Creator. Its beauty still holds us spellbound!

It may be harsh and stark and forbidding. But it holds a fascination that can't be explained. It's the crisp, clean air. It's the wide panorama of mountain peaks. It's the gnarled trees that cling to the rocks on the bare edge of existence. It's the stately forests below you. It's walking where yours are the only footprints. It's back-packing beyond the trail's end. It's riding your horse through the rocky crags and stopping to rest for a moment—wishing your eyes had been the first ever to take in the wide sweep of the Sierra. It's looking down at the ground and seeing, close by your horse's hoof, a fragile little flower not two inches high, blooming safe and unafraid!

There's a tiny blue flower that blooms on the upper heights. It's called the sky pilot—after the slang term for a chaplain, or one who shows the way to heaven.

So it is, or ought to be, with all the high country. It ought to call us, urge us, attract us to a better land. A land where there are flowers that never fade. A land where there are rivers— especially the river of life. A land where there are trees—and best of all, the tree of life. A land where the wildlife are all unafraid. A land where there is no sickness or heartache. A land where there are no tears, no sorrow, and no death. A land where there is no night. A land where there are no goodbyes. A land where you can talk face to face with the Creator of it all!

Try to picture what God's high country must be like. If even in stark disarray His creation is as beautiful as what we see today, what must it have been before it was catapulted into wild confusion? What must the original have been—if the torn and twisted remainder is like this?

Even as we see it today, we may be tempted to say, "Heaven can wait. I want to stay here."

But did you know that God has in mind our staying here— after we've had a taste of heaven, after we've spent a thousand happy years there. Did you know that this earth, not heaven, is to be our permanent home? Jesus said, "The meek . . . shall inherit the earth." Matthew 5:5, KJV.

Remember? And the apostle Peter says, "In keeping with his promise we are looking forward to a new heaven and a new earth." 2 Peter 3:13, KJV.

God is going to burn away the scars from this earth—and give it back to us new. All new. Everything new!

Try to imagine the majesty, the breathtaking loveliness of God's high country—without the scars! Imagine what it will be to share it with those to whom you'll never have to say goodbye!

The scars will be all gone. Says the prophet Isaiah:

"The wilderness and the solitary place shall . . . blossom as the rose. It shall blossom abundantly, and . . . the glory of Lebanon shall be given unto it . . . for in the wilderness shall waters break out, and streams in the desert." Isaiah 25:1-6, KJV.

Streams in the desert. Says an inspired pen, "There are ever-flowing streams, clear as crystal, and beside them waving trees cast their shadows upon the paths prepared for the ransomed of the Lord. There the wide-spreading plains swell into hills of beauty, and the mountains of God rear their lofty summits. On those peaceful plains, beside those living streams, God's people, so long pilgrims and wanderers, shall find a home."

Think of it, friend! Think of this earth when God makes it new and gives it back to us in its original beauty. The mountains crowned with stately trees. The canyons, the waterfalls, the lakes, the grand sweep of an untarnished creation all around you. Yet nothing stark or bare or forbidding. Nothing desolate or lonely. And God's high country will be yours to keep—forever as fresh and lovely as if it had never been touched!

Forever, if you choose, you will be free to probe vast areas where your footsteps are the first to leave their print upon the yielding soil. There beside your horse's hoofs will grow delicate flowers—so infinitely small as contrasted with the towering peaks, yet equally safe in the hands of a loving God!

I want to be there! Don't you?

God and the Cities

It was shortly after 2:00 a.m. James Hopper, his copy ready for the next edition of the *Call*, was on his way home. The breeze from the sea was losing force, and the night seemed particularly peaceful.

As he passed a livery stable between Powell and Mason, he heard the sudden shrill scream of a horse. Poking his head into the darkened doorway, he was met by the thunder of a score of hoofs crashing against the stalls.

"Restless tonight," the stableman explained. "Don't know why."

James Hopper continued uphill. Restless horses. Must be the weather.

At the same moment, making the rounds of the city's night spots, Enrico Caruso, the famed tenor, was restless too—restless, and yet confident of what the day's reviews would say of his flawless performance of the evening.

Dennis Sullivan, the city fire chief, had been worried since the first fire call came in shortly after midnight. The wind had veered. It was now gusting off the Pacific. And every time the heart of the city had burned, the wind had come from the sea.

So the night passed.

A little before five, Police Officer Leonard Ingham awoke. For two months now he had been having nightmares. And his dreams were always the same. Always the fire swept up Market Street, and then across it, gutting with its hot breath the city's principal buildings. And then, out of control, it would

193

push masses of frightened humanity before it into the sea.

But tonight he had had no nightmare. Perhaps that was because he had made an appointment for this very morning to tell Jeremiah Dinan, the police chief, his dreams. Strange, though. The milkman, rattling his cart along the street at that moment, was having trouble trying to quiet his excited horse.

The city clocks struck 5:00 a.m.

Bailey Millard, from the terrace of his villa atop Russian Hill, was at his easel again, hoping to capture on canvas the gray-green fascination of an awakening city. He would begin with Telegraph Hill.

Nothing anywhere seemed to stir. He started to paint.

And Jessie Cook, a police sergeant on patrol in the produce district, noticed that the clock on the Ferry Building said 5:14. It was fast. It was only 5:12 by his watch.

Time hung poised over the city of San Francisco. It was Wednesday, April 18, 1906.

And then it happened.

"It came out of the sea at seven thousand miles an hour, almost directly beneath the lighthouse on Point Arena, ninety miles north," say those who know the story best.

And then "relentlessly the rip raced south, veering when it met the resistance of the land, but keeping the same general direction, boring down toward San Francisco, shifting billions of tons of earth, sending masses of rock rising and falling to form cliffs where only a second before there had been flat land."

Bailey Millard, high on Russian Hill, his easel smashed and his paints scattered, watched it all. The tall, proud buildings were swaying and rocking. Brick walls crashed. Towers and cornices toppled. The skyline was dancing, and it seemed to him that City Hall was leading the dance.

It was as if San Francisco were being pushed into the sea. And the tower bell of Old St. Mary's Church in Chinatown, clanging senselessly, seemed to him, and to others, to be tolling like a mighty bell—tolling Judgment Day for a city that deserved it.

The shaking stopped. And then the fires came. And confusion.

A woman sat on the sidewalk toying with a pair of shoes. Another carried a baby upside down by its heels, as if it were a turkey. An undertaker squatted in front of his funeral parlor, quietly polishing coffin handles.

In Chinatown, the street was packed with coolies and merchants and children, many of them shouting at a huge brown bull that lurched among them, frightened and in pain. They had been taught, some of them, that the world was supported on the backs of four bulls. This must be one of them.

"Go back! Bull, go back!" they shouted. "Your brothers need you under the world!"

And Enrico Caruso had managed to take the earthquake personally. He was sure it was intended just for him. He sat bolt upright in his bed in the Palace Hotel. The earthquake had piled his forty pairs of boots, along with all his dressing gowns and silk shirts, into the fireplace. He wept hysterically, absolutely certain that his voice was damaged, gone.

His conductor, trying to comfort him, asked if he had tried it. Then opening the window wide, he rapped his baton on the window sill and commanded the tenor to sing. He did. At the top of his voice.

And in the confused crowd below the window, there were those who interrupted their own personal panic to listen, and to say how brave he was. At least Caruso was not afraid!

But he was. And San Francisco was. And it still is.

It will happen again, they say. And when it does, they say it may "come as it did in April 1906—unexpectedly, rushing up from the Pacific seabed, rippling south at over seven thousand miles an hour, preceded by an uncommonly warm day."

Tolling like a mighty bell over a planet in rebellion is the call of a lonely Creator—a Creator who will never be satisfied until man comes home. If you listen closely, you can hear it in the low rumble of approaching catastrophe. You can feel it in the nervous quaking of the earth. You can sense it in the evening news.

It rings out over the cities where men crowd together to gain some comfort, however temporary, in the warmth of neon and the supposed security of steel. It echoes in the hills and valleys where men seek to escape what seems to be an ominous rush to oblivion. It has never been completely quieted in the hearts of men and women.

The tolling bell is the sound of loneliness—the echo of man's own heartbeat. For man, however reluctant to acknowledge his Creator, however arrogant his profession of unbelief, seems to sense that he is lost—and lonely—and needs to be found.

The bell still tolls. Perhaps you can hear it best over the cities.

There are sophisticated cities, laughing cities, cities of sorrow. Cities of sin. Dead cities like Petra, and surprised cities like Pompeii. Nineveh, the city that repented.

There are 20th-century cities—proud, reckless, driving. Hard and harsh and masculine like New York—or Chicago. Teeming, throbbing London. Tense, sensitive, nervous cities like today's Jerusalem. And frightened San Francisco.

Could it be that in God's dealing with the cities we could better understand how God feels about this planet in rebellion?

Cities, you see, are like people. They live, they breathe, they die like human beings. They may be dressed in brick and mortar, stone and steel, but they beat with a heart. And God deals with the heart!

Have you ever stopped to think how much there is at stake? Do you realize how slender the thread of survival really is in our great cities?

No spot is more vulnerable to devastating enemy attack, to the failure of mechanical devices, or to the tricks of weather, than New York and its metropolitan rivals. A little fog is enough to immobilize a city. A little frozen rain on its streets, and it is crippled. And no city is a match for a hurricane or a volcano.

Yes, it's a slender thread. And there is more at stake than we realize.

Come with me, then, to the cities of the past. It may be we can discover how God feels about the cities of today—and what He will do with them.

Take, for instance, the city of Nineveh, one of the earliest centers of population. It was the capital of Assyria, no doubt the most feared empire of all history.

Nineveh today is but a vast, irregular rectangle of mounds lying near Mosul on the left bank of the Tigris River. And as we stood on the central mound with our IT IS WRITTEN cameras and panned the outlines of Nineveh, I realized why God called it a "great city." For those ancient walls in the distance, a circuit of seven and a half miles, encompassed nearly 1800 acres of land.

Scholars have been able to recover a little of Nineveh's original magnificence. For example, they found in Sennacherib's palace no less than seventy-one halls, chambers, and passages whose walls, almost without exception, had been paneled with sculptured slabs of alabaster. And we think we have arrived!

It was to this politically strong and powerful seat of empire that God dispatched Jonah on one of the greatest missions of mercy ever recorded. And of course the story of Jonah's procrastination is familiar to most everyone. But when he finally arrived, after a most unusual detour, how he did preach! And how Nineveh listened!

His message was a clear, simple call to repentance. "Forty days from now Nineveh will be destroyed." Jonah 3:4, LB.

Nineveh listened. Nineveh repented. Nineveh tells me that a city that will hear the voice of God is a city saved—just as Sodom tells me that a city that will not hear the voice of God is a city lost.

Tolling like a mighty bell through all the Scriptures is the word *repent*. That word stands like a gigantic backdrop in the drama of the ages. It is God's call to the human heart.

Jonah had penetrated only a third of the way into the great metropolis. But the word spread, conviction deepened, and the city, from the king to the humblest servant, repented. And God withheld His hand.

What a record! What a story! Nineveh is remembered today, not as the mighty city it was, not for its slabs of alabaster, but as the city that repented. And it is a living encouragement to all who read the record.

Babylon is not so remembered. Babylon was indeed a mighty city, even by modern standards. Its hanging gardens are still classed as one of the seven wonders of the ancient world. In fact, it lay in the midst of a valley so productive that one historian feared he would be considered a liar if he reported what he actually saw. From a human standpoint nothing could prevent it from continuing indefinitely.

Yet even before Babylon had reached the peak of its power, the prophet Isaiah predicted its overthrow. "And so Babylon, the most glorious of kingdoms, the flower of Chaldean culture, will be as utterly destroyed as Sodom and Gomorrah were when God sent fire from heaven; Babylon will never rise again. Generation after generation will come and go, but the land will never again be lived in. The nomads will not even camp there. The shepherds won't let their sheep stay overnight." Isaiah 13:19, 20, LB.

But Babylon was to be warned. It was to have a chance to avert this tragedy. God had used a humble preacher to warn Nineveh. Babylon was to have the witness and example of a prophet-statesman standing fearlessly in the highest circles of the empire.

You remember the story. Young Daniel, a captive of Judah, was lifted from slavery to stand next to the king. And God prepared him for his mission. God was going to speak to the heart of Babylon—and win it if he could!

Babylon was rocked by the voice of God through its prime minister—rocked, but not won. At last came the handwriting on the wall—and God wrote across the name of Babylon, "You have been weighed in God's balances and have failed the test." Daniel 5:27, LB.

Nineveh rises to memory in vindication of the word *repent*. But Babylon goes down forever a pitiful example of love spurned too long.

I suppose that one of the most intriguing cities of all past history was Petra—the ancient capital of the Edomites. Carved out of solid rock, its perpendicular cliffs of red sandstone formed a perfect barrier to invading forces through many centuries of colorful experience. Into those red sandstone mountains were carved palaces, tombs, and temples—and the stairs that led to the high altars of sun worship, with its revolting immorality.

Yet Petra had its chance to repent. To the north was a small, unpopular kingdom with only a fraction of Petra's wealth and power, but within whose borders the God of the nations chose to dwell. Israel was an imperfect, faltering witness, to be sure. But Petra might have heard. Instead, Petra today is only a dead caricature of a forgotten past.

Then Jerusalem—historic, loved and lovable Jerusalem. I suppose that no city on earth ever heard such earnest and faithful appeals from the actual lips of the Saviour as did Jerusalem.

I can never shake off the impression of the day when Jesus interrupted His own triumphal entry into Jerusalem to look out over the city from the Mount of Olives. The western sun was lighting up the pure white marble of the temple walls and sparkling on its gold-capped pillars. And suddenly, like a note of wailing in a grand triumphal chorus, Jesus wept.

Evidently into one crowded moment swept the memory of the banker, the carpenter, the housewife, the priest—those who had listened and been deeply moved by His ministry, whose sicknesses had been healed, but who yet would reject Him. These were Jerusalem. It was the sight of Jerusalem that caused the Son of God to weep. He had come to save her. How could He let her go?

He was soon to leave her temple for the last time. He would cast one lingering look upon its marble walls and then exclaim, "O Jerusalem, Jerusalem, the city that kills the prophets, and stones all those God sends to her! How often I have wanted to gather your children together as a hen gathers her chicks beneath her wings, but you wouldn't let me." Matthew 23:37, LB.

This was the separation struggle. This was the mysterious farewell of indestructible love to a city that would not repent!

I think I can understand a little of our Lord's concern on that day. For my most helpless moments are when I confront a nominal Christian in a man-to-man appeal for absolute committal to the Saviour, for complete abandon to Christ—and then see that half-converted heart close like a steel door and turn indifferently away.

Compare this, if you will, with the man or woman who faces the claims of Christ under deep conviction of guilt, and finds his way to forgiveness. No wonder all heaven rejoices when one sinner repents.

Jerusalem tells me that nothing, absolutely nothing, is more deceiving than the subtle immunity that comes with the belief that a man is all right because of an outward profession of Christianity—no matter how superficial his contact with Christ may be. No man is more dangerously situated than the half-hearted Christian who is too proud to repent!

Too proud to repent! Could this be the reason Jerusalem has experienced so confused and contradictory a history? Today it is the enigma of nations, the most perplexing city in the world— tense, nervous, explosive, a vortex of intrigue.

But now for a moment we turn to the silent, sleeping city of Pompeii—a mute reminder of the deadly danger of procrastination. Deadlines have always been final. But the deadline of 1:00 p.m., August 24, A.D. 79, was as final as the last night on earth.

I cannot walk through the silent streets of Pompeii without realizing that it spent its last night in defying its God. What a man sees there makes that city an illustration forever of reckless, head-on rebellion.

Did God send no voice to warn Pompeii? He must have. Of one thing we can be certain. God did not forget that proud, sophisticated city. He did not permit her to breathe the deadly fumes of Vesuvius until she had heard the word *repent*.

The Spirit of God must have pleaded most earnestly with Pompeii on that last night. The Spirit always speaks most loudly just before a man, or a city, is forever cut off.

But the hour of separation does come. There is a line beyond which even divine love cannot go. God says, "My Spirit shall not always strive with man."

But today, still tolling like a mighty bell over the cities is the call of God, "Repent!" And the bell tolls loudest just before it is forever silenced.

Will God permit our cities—our proud, reckless, driving cities—to fall? Was Hiroshima only the first of a long line of casualties of this atomic age? No sober man these days doubts the possibility. And God says it will happen. It will happen in our day. Listen to Revelation! "And the cities of the nations fell."

The cities will fall. God will touch the cities. And the finest, most fireproof buildings will crumble like the ashes on the end of a cigarette. Buildings perfectly safe, by modern standards. But they will be consumed like pitch. Fire departments will be helpless when God allows the fires of judgment to be lighted.

That is what makes me restless. There is so little time—and so much at stake!

The bell still tolls, "Repent! Repent! Repent!" It is the Jonah of today for the Ninevehs of today. It is the Daniel of today for the Babylons of today. It is the rumbling of Vesuvius for the Pompeiis of today. It is Christ weeping over the Jerusalems of today. The bell still tolls. But it is God's last call!

God is reckoning with the cities. And you—and I—we are the cities! Oh Detroit, with your humming dynamos, with your idols of steel and chrome, God says "Repent!" New York, with your jungles of cement, with your long fingers of light reaching high into the sky, God says, "Repent!" Washington, with your graceful avenues, with your equitable system of justice, with your government for the people and by the people, God says, "Repent!" San Francisco, Los Angeles, London, Paris, Tokyo, spattering your streets and your skies with crimson neon, God says, "Repent!"

"And the cities of the nations fell."

Where will you stand when the bell tolls no longer, when never another heart will be moved, never another mind impressed, when the God of heaven says, "He that is unjust, let him be unjust still . . . and he that is righteous, let him be righteous still: and he that is holy, let him be holy still. And, behold, I come quickly."

Where will you be when a rejected Saviour calls out in inconceivable disappointment, "O strange planet in rebellion, how long and patiently I have knocked at your towers of glass and urged you to let Me in; I would have saved you from the burning, but you would not"?

Today—just now—the bell still tolls! Will you pray this prayer with me?

Dear God, that bell tolls for me. I am the one. I am the one that needs help. Grant me repentance, and give me the humility and the grace to receive it. Prepare me in this day of decision. I want above all else to be on the Lord's side. I earnestly ask this in Jesus' saving name. Amen.

Hoax or History?

A Man named Jesus told His friends one day that on a visit to the city of Jerusalem He would be killed by His enemies. But He claimed to have power over death!

Did He?

What about the resurrection of Jesus of Nazareth? Was it a heartless hoax? Or was it the most fantastic fact of history?

It was one or the other!

If ever anybody went out on a limb, Jesus did. Not once, but many times, He talked about His coming death—and said He would rise again. He even made an appointment to meet His friends after His resurrection!

But it simply didn't register in the minds of His followers. They were so consumed with optimism about the coming kingdom they thought He was about set up—and their status in it—that their minds were closed to any thought of harm coming to Him.

Now, of course if Jesus really was the Son of God, as He claimed to be, you would *expect* Him to have power over death. Wouldn't you?

In fact, all the miracles of Christ's life, all the profound yet simple teaching, all the holy living, all the healing, all the promises—these wouldn't mean a thing if He didn't have power over death. You can trace it all and marvel at it all. You can be convinced by it all. You can even be drawn by it all. But if Jesus of Nazareth died like any other man and that was the end of Him, then we might just as well forget about Him!

Either He was God or He wasn't. If He was, even death would have to obey His command. He could lay down His life of His own free will. And He could also take it up again of His own free will!

If Jesus was only a human being, if He was only a martyr dying for a good cause, if what happened that day outside Jerusalem was only another murder, another crucifixion among the thousands of Roman crucifixions—then this world today is darker than anybody thinks. And that's pretty dark!

You see, Christianity stands or falls with the resurrection of Christ. Without the resurrection, Christianity is only another system of ethics. Helpful perhaps. Comfortable perhaps. But not saving!

The one big difference between Christianity and other religions is the empty tomb!

I have watched the rituals of Hinduism in India—rituals that range from the horrible to the sublime. In these Eastern lands, in seemingly endless forms, I saw men desperately seeking for peace and inner cleansing. Hoping that they had found it—or that someday they would make the discovery.

They were sincere. They were dedicated. They were deeply in earnest. But there was no empty tomb!

I saw Buddhism, with its yellow-robed monks and palm-leaf umbrellas, with its prayer wheels and elaborate ritual. More than a quarter of a billion people seek to find the answers in that meditative and passive religion.

Devotion? Yes. But no empty tomb!

I have observed the philosophies of China, the ethical teachings of Confucius and Lao-tzu and Mao. But behind the color and pageantry and the wisdom in a little red book there is an inner hunger.

Why? Because there is no empty tomb!

I have traveled through the world of Islam, with its submission, with its prophet, spanning half the globe. I have talked with these followers of Mohammed and seen their burning sincerity and unashamed devotion.

But I never saw an empty tomb!

I have walked the soil of Palestine. I saw the descendants of

Abraham, justly proud of their heritage as keepers of the law. The empty tomb is right there among them. But few have recognized the Man who said He would walk out of it—and did!

I wish I could lead them all, and lead *you* all, along Jerusalem's streets, along the Via Dolorosa, the way of the cross, out past Calvary to the garden tomb that many believe to be most like the one from which our Lord stepped out that morning 1900 years ago.

I have stood beside it a number of times. I have stepped inside—and felt again the difference between Christianity and every other religion. That tomb has no occupant! That's the difference! The man who rested there briefly stepped out of it in three days! And He said, "I am the resurrection, and the life!"

Confucius couldn't say that! Buddha couldn't say that! Mohammed couldn't say that! Abraham couldn't say that!

The tomb of Confucius is occupied. The tomb of the Buddha is occupied. The tomb of Mohammed is occupied.

But the tomb of Jesus Christ is empty! There isn't a shrine in the world that claims one bone of the body of the Son of God. He left death eternally behind that day—and left an empty tomb as a witness!

Friend, if you're looking for certainty, here it is!

But now suppose we ask, Just *how* certain is the resurrection? Just *how* sure can we be?

True, it was the resurrection that led a mere handful of men, most of them uneducated, all of them persecuted and hunted and harassed, to turn a pagan world upside down. It was the resurrection that did it. Those men went out and transformed a pagan society—not by argument, but by their flaming testimony of a risen Lord! They gladly gave their lives because they thought it was true!

Listen! Men may think a lie, or propagate a lie. They may speak a lie or print a lie or shout a lie or prophesy a lie. But they don't die for what they *know* is a lie!

But is it possible that it wasn't true after all? Could they have been deluded? Honest, but mistaken? Possibly the unwitting victims of some trick—or some convincing hallucination?

What if the resurrection story was all a carefully contrived hoax? Or a legend that has gathered sacredness with the centuries until now we think it really happened?

You see, going to church on Easter Sunday is one thing. It's not much of a risk. Its total cost may be the price of a spring suit you would buy anyway, plus a gallon of gas and five dollars in the collection plate.

But suppose one of these days the way gets rough and Jesus isn't as popular as He is today. Suppose we in this favored land should be hunted and persecuted and harassed because of our faith in a risen Lord. Suppose doubts are shouted at you from every side—and you realize that to speak just one word against Jesus could get you out of trouble or even save your life. What then?

Are we certain—really certain—about the resurrection? Certain enough to see us through a day like that? Because we might as well forget our faith in Christ if the resurrection isn't true. It doesn't matter how many other things we are certain about. It all falls if the resurrection falls!

Suppose we backtrack just a little in the life of Jesus. His whole life was an evidence that He was who He said He was. The miracles. The teaching. The life He lived. The healing. The compassion. The love.

And then there were the prophecies fulfilled in His life and in His death. They are evidence that no man can escape. Prophecies concerning His birth, prophecies about His ministry, about His death. Someone has estimated that more than 300 Old Testament prophecies were made—and all fulfilled—in Jesus. Was it just an accident? Was it just coincidence?

Oh, you might find one or two fulfilled in some other man somewhere. I don't know. But the possibility of their all being fulfilled in one man by chance or by accident or by coincidence is so small as to stagger the mind!

It has been suggested by one doubter that Jesus simply maneuvered the fulfillment of all these prophecies, that He followed them like a blueprint and lived them out in order to strengthen His claims.

Well, could Jesus control the time of His birth or the manner of His birth? Or the place of His birth? Could He control the manner of His death? Did He bribe the Roman soldiers to gamble over His robe to fulfill a prophecy? Did He call for a Roman soldier to pierce His side and see if He was dead? Did He select the place where they laid Him to rest? Hardly!

Peter Stoner, in the book *Science Speaks*, shows that coincidence is ruled out by the science of probability!

He takes just eight out of the 300 prophecies concerning Jesus that were fulfilled—just eight, mind you—and finds that the chance of these eight prophecies being fulfilled in any one man is only one in 10^{17}. That would be one in 100,000,000,000,000,000!

And now listen to this. To help us understand such a staggering figure, Peter Stoner illustrates by supposing that we take 10^{17} silver dollars and lay them on the face of Texas. They will cover all of the state two feet deep. Now mark one of these silver dollars and stir the whole mass thoroughly, all over the state. Blindfold a man and tell him that he can travel all over Texas if he wishes, but he must pick up the one particular silver dollar that was marked!

What chance would he have of picking the right one on the first try? Just the same chance the prophets had—if they wrote only in their own wisdom! And we've considered only eight prophecies! What chance would there be with 300? Evidently we can be very certain that Jesus was who He said He was!

But wait! In spite of His faultless life, in spite of His incomparable teaching, in spite of all the miracles, in spite of all the prophecies fulfilled—it all narrows down to this. It all stands or falls with one question. Did this man Jesus have power over death? Did He walk out of that tomb?

If He didn't, He was the greatest impostor this world has ever seen. If He claimed to be God but couldn't conquer death, then it is all a heartless hoax. And all this mountain of evidence in other areas doesn't add a thing to His claims—but only to the enormity of the deception!

For what good would there be in a God who promised life but couldn't keep His promise? In a cross that could forgive but could not save? In a gospel limited to the past—without any future?

Jesus said, "I am the living one; for I was dead and now I am alive for evermore, and I hold the keys of Death and Death's domain." Revelation 1:19, NEB.

Did He tell the truth? I believe He did!

Most of us know the resurrection story only as it is told in the Bible. Few of us have taken the time to search the pages of history to see what they have to say about the resurrection of Jesus of Nazareth. Few of us have read the admissions of the skeptics, forced from unwilling lips.

Let me tell you this. You would be absolutely amazed at what you would find—at the mountain of evidence. I'm not going to give it to you here—I wouldn't know where to begin. But I've been reading some of it recently, and I'm still standing in wonder at what I found. More than one skeptic has set out to disprove the resurrection—only to end up a devoted disciple of the living Christ. That empty tomb stands there in history for all to see—like a mighty Gibraltar that cannot be moved!

Josh McDowell, once a skeptic himself, was asked by a university student, "Professor McDowell, why can't you refute Christianity?"

He answered, "For a very simple reason. I am not able to explain away an event in history—the resurrection of Jesus Christ."

Suppose we get the picture in mind—the scene as that Saturday night wore on toward morning.

Jesus was dead. He was in the tomb. A great stone had been rolled in front of its entrance. That stone was sealed with the Roman seal. And a Roman guard stood watch—with death the penalty for sleep!

The disciples of Jesus? They were in hiding, their hopes crushed.

Then suddenly the tomb was empty. Inside sat an angel, who said to the sorrowing women at dawn, "He is not here: for he is risen!"

Wonderful words! Tremendous words! No greater words were ever spoken. He is not here! He is risen!

In those words is the only hope for the human race. Your only hope—and mine. And thank God, no skeptic has ever been able to prove them untrue!

But it isn't because they haven't tried!

Some, of course, are unwilling to believe even when the evidence blazes like the sun at noon. And they have come up with theories of their own about what happened that Sunday morning. I think we ought to examine some of them. I believe it would strengthen our faith.

First of all, of course, there is the story put in the mouths of the Roman guard by the Jewish leaders when they learned that Jesus had risen. "Some of the guard went into the city and reported to the chief priests everything that had happened. After meeting with the elders and conferring together, the chief priests offered the soldiers a substantial bribe and told them to say, 'His disciples came by night and stole the body while we were asleep.' . . . So they took the money and did as they were told." Matthew 28:11-15, NEB.

That was a self-contradicting story, of course. Because if they were asleep, how did they know what had happened? It tells more about the frustration of the priests than anything else!

No. Those Roman soldiers were not sleeping. The penalty for sleeping at their post was death—and it was strictly enforced. And even if one of them had succumbed to drowsiness, would they all have been asleep?

And if all were asleep and were awakened to see the disciples robbing the tomb—and how else could they have known?—how easy it would have been for those powerful Roman soldiers to overcome a few frightened, unarmed disciples! They could have taken them easily into custody—and the body too!

And about that stone at the entrance to the tomb. Here is something interesting. I understand that those who made the copies of the Scriptures were not permitted to insert any thought of their own, or emphasize any point, in the text itself. But they were permitted to write an observation into the margin.

In one ancient manuscript these words concerning the stone appear in the margin: "a stone which twenty men could not roll away." An observation that likely originated with someone who had seen the stone and been impressed with the size and weight of it!

Do you think for a moment that a few disciples could have rolled away a stone like that—and all without awakening the sleeping soldiers?

The soldiers knew what had happened. They saw it all. They saw an angel sweep earthward and roll away the stone as if it were a pebble—not slowed a moment by the Roman seal! They saw the Son of God walk out of the tomb and proclaim over it, "I am the resurrection, and the life!" They were too excited, too awed, to report to the priests anything but the truth!

The Jewish leaders didn't doubt their story. They didn't even visit the tomb to verify it. Why didn't they launch a massive FBI investigation and produce the body? That would have put an end to Christianity before it was born!

There are still those who suggest that the resurrection was all a hoax contrived in the minds of the disciples. But were frightened, scared men who were hidden away in an upper room for fear of the Jews, men who didn't believe the news of the resurrection even where they were told it, men who thought their faith in Jesus had all been a mistake after all— were they in any mood to contrive a hoax? Hardly!

Some say the women that morning were so blinded by darkness and tears that they came to the wrong tomb—that Jesus was really lying dead in a tomb nearby.

But would the angel have been mistaken about which tomb it was?

If the empty tomb was the wrong tomb, it should have been easy enough to find the right one nearby and produce the body. Searching a few tombs at the edge of Jerusalem would have been infinitely easy compared to searching caves surrounding the Dead Sea for scrolls.

There are those who say that Jesus did not really die on the cross, that He only swooned, and afterward revived.

No. Jesus was really dead. The thrust of the spear, and the flow of blood and water that followed, left no doubt. And medical science tells us that such a flow of blood and water is exactly what we would expect in the case of a crucifixion where the victim had died of a ruptured heart. And He did. He died of a broken heart!

Are we to suppose that a Man who had been tortured and abused, without food for many hours, a Man who had been near death in Gethsemane and who couldn't carry His cross, would revive in a closed-up cave?

Are we to suppose that He could have performed the superhuman feat of rolling that stone away—and all without disturbing the soldiers? And then walked away on wounded feet?

No. Not a single alternative to the resurrection has been offered that is either credible or sane. As we probe the story of the empty tomb, it is the frustrated silence of the enemies of Christ, their utter inability to explain it away, that speaks loudest of all. That silence is deafening!

Do you see what God has done? Knowing the supreme importance of the resurrection, knowing that all else hinges upon it, and knowing the attacks that would be aimed against it—God has tightly closed every loophole, every niche that might give entry to uncertainty. He wants us to be sure! And yet being convinced is not enough. Acknowledging the evidence is not enough. Conviction and commitment are not the same thing.

Pilate heard that Christ had risen. And it troubled him till the moment of his death. But it did not save him. The religious leaders knew it was true—but only tried to control the news. Knowledge didn't change their hearts!

Thomas heard it—and *didn't* believe it. But when he saw the evidence in the Saviour's hands, he changed his mind. He knelt at His feet in worship!

A small band of followers examined the evidence and not only believed but acted upon it. And the resurrection stamped their faith with a certainty that was willing to face death!

That same certainty can be yours as you are reading the final pages of this book. There is no better time than now to rest your whole weight on—to place your entire confidence in—the Lord Jesus Christ, your Savior and mine. He can be trusted. You can be certain of that.

Five Kilometers East

Two travelers, weary beyond words, were crossing the desert in the stifling heat. Their water supply was exhausted. They were pushing ahead with borrowed strength. And how much more would nature let them borrow? Their minds were discussing surrender to the sandy killer of men.

And then, at the farthest reach of their vision, their eyes latched onto a tiny patch of green. Could it be a mirage? No. It was real. The patch of green was larger now and more distinct. Something was growing there. And whatever it was, it was evidently getting water.

Water! The thought of it gave them courage to push on. It must be an oasis!

Using what must be the last of their strength, they dragged themselves into the haven of green. And there before their eyes, in this paradise of shade, was a well! And beside it a wooden bucket!

Hurriedly, expectantly, they let down the bucket. But it landed with a thud! The well was dry!

This was too much! They might as well just lie down in the cool, comfortable shade and admit that the desert had won!

And then they saw something else. A few feet away from the well, on the ground, was a piece of board. Someone, with a knife or some sharp instrument, had carved words into it. It said: WATER—FIVE KILOMETERS EAST.

Water! Five kilometers! Could they possibly make it? Could they summon up a few more ounces of strength? Of course they could. And did. Who would choose to lie down and die, even in cool comfort, with water only five kilometers away?

What about *living* water? Would we walk five kilometers for it? Or would we settle into the short-range comfort of a dry well and refuse to budge?

A woman of Samaria, you remember, met Jesus at Jacob's well one hot noon. He offered her living water. And she became so excited that she forgot her waterpot and went to call her friends.

Abraham heard the call of God one day. He left his comfortable home and began a long walk that was still unfinished when he died.

Three wise men from a distant country followed a star for many a night to find the newborn King.

But the Pharisees in the days of Jesus were satisfied, content, and even proud of their dry wells. They decided to stay right where they were. They were quite comfortable in their situation. And they had enough self-manufactured shade to keep the light of truth from shining too brightly in their eyes.

Dry wells haven't *always* been dry. At some time or other they have yielded enough water to produce some flourishing vegetation—enough living green to attract weary travelers and lead them to linger nearby.

But if you discover that the well on which you depend has gone dry, there is only one thing to do. Move! Find another well! Five kilometers away—or five hundred!

Things change in this deteriorating world of ours. Respectable neighborhoods become slums. Shiny new cars on the showroom floor are one day hauled away as junk. Roses are replaced with weeds. Wells go dry. And worship, once sincere, becomes only a hollow form!

Religion is especially vulnerable to the deteriorating influences of our day. Everything about our practice of religion is susceptible to the inroads of compromise and carelessness. Principles are abandoned little by little. Religious groups once pledged to follow the Bible and the Bible only—willing to die for it—have reasoned it away a little at a time until they find themselves holding tightly to nothing but tradition. Ministers who used to preach the gospel of Jesus Christ have turned to preaching politics and protest. And many a worshiper, when suddenly he discovers that the well is dry, is stunned!

Edward Gibbon, writing in his *Decline and Fall of the Roman Empire*, was describing how the zeal of ancient Rome faded after Caesar's armies had subdued the world and later generations were left with the inheritance of their fathers. And he penned these memorable words: "They held in their lifeless hands the riches of their fathers without inheriting the spirit which had created and improved that sacred patrimony. They read, they compiled, but their languor of soul seemed incapable of thought and action."

It can happen to a nation. Could it happen to a church? Could a church hold in its hands millions of dollars worth of buildings—without inheriting the spirit of the pioneers who built them?

Never was there a people more missionary-minded than the Waldenses. Remember them? For many centuries during the dark ages of persecution they worshiped their Lord in the Piedmont valleys of northern Italy, protected by the lofty mountains about them. Early in life they were taught their mission. They copied the Scriptures by hand. And then they went out, disguised as merchants or peddlers, the precious manuscripts of the Bible hidden in their clothing. They went into the cities, into the universities, into the homes. Cautiously the missionary would produce a portion of the Scriptures. And then, with quivering lip and on bended knee, he would read the precious promises. Often he would be asked to read them again and again. Could it be true that "the blood of Jesus Christ his Son cleanseth us from all sin"? As light dawned upon their troubled minds, they would exclaim, "Christ is my priest! His blood is my sacrifice!"

Sometimes the entire night was spent in this manner. The assurance of a Saviour's love seemed too good to be true. They would ask, "Will God accept *my* offering? Will He pardon *me*?"

The answer would be read again from Scripture, until the understanding could grasp it. And the response would come, "I may come to Jesus just as I am, sinful and unholy. 'Thy sins be forgiven thee.' *Mine, even mine,* may be forgiven!"

Joy filled the heart. All fear of prison or flame now was gone. They would gladly welcome death, if it would honor their Lord!

The messenger of truth went on his way, in many cases to be seen no more. He had made his way to other lands. Or he was wearing out his life in some unknown dungeon. Or perhaps his bones were left whitening on the spot where he had witnessed for his Lord. Such was the grand and untarnished devotion of the Waldenses!

But there is a sad postscript to that story. Not many years ago, near the little Waldensian village of Torre Pellice, a group of Christian youth gathered around their campfire to sing gospel songs and to tell mission stories.

Visitors from the surrounding valleys and mountains had drifted into the village, and now they approached the campfire with curiosity. Who were these young people? They heard them praying. They heard them singing about the second coming of Jesus, in which their own fathers had once so ardently believed. They heard them telling mission stories, and it brought a strange nostalgia for their own past.

On this night, after the singing and the stories were over, one of the Waldensian elders stepped from the shadows into the light of the campfire and spoke thoughtfully to the minister in charge, "*You must carry on!*"

And he continued, "We, the Waldensian people, have a great heritage behind us. We are proud of the history of our people as they have fought to preserve the light of truth high upon these mountaintops and up and down these valleys. This is our home. Here we have the great monuments of our faith. . . . Of all this we are proud."

And then this Waldensian elder, a layman in the church, said with conviction, "This is our great heritage of the past, but we really do not have any future. We have given up the teachings in which we once believed. We no longer believe that Jesus will soon come in the clouds of heaven. This belief we have abandoned. From all that I can observe, from what I have heard about your people, *you* must now carry on!"

And then he pointed to a nearby mountain. "If you look up

here on the mountainside, you will see one of our Waldensian chapels. You will notice on this chapel, as on all our chapels, these words: . . . 'And the light shineth in darkness!' . . . But now beside these chapels we have built dance halls, thinking that in this way we might be able to hold our young people.

"Yet our young people seem to have no more interest in, or love for, the church. Their interest now is down in the bright lights of the big cities. No longer do they want to remain here.

"What a miracle it is that you still have young people who are interested in coming up here to our valley and in studying the history we love so much. But that is all in the past now. The sad thing is that we are not moving forward with courage for the future. *You* must carry on!"

Such is the haunting appeal of the Waldenses!

What a tragedy it is to stagnate, to fall asleep, to stand still when we might be moving into a future far brighter than the past! What a tragedy to abandon our beliefs—or water them down until we don't know what they are!

Not long ago a group of student leaders from across America were called to the White House. A government spokesman, in a carefully prepared speech, told them to be good students—not to bomb buildings, not to skip the country, not to give up on America. When he had finished, a student from Harvard stood and asked on what grounds these moral concepts were founded.

The official stood for a moment, flushed and embarrassed. Then he replied apologetically, "I'm sorry. I don't know."

Doesn't it make you wonder how many of our concepts today have no solid foundation? Is it possible that many of our popularly accepted beliefs are nothing but speculation—or nothing but tradition?

A few years back one of our airlines ran a two-page ad. Across the top it said this: "For 25 years you've been brainwashed into expecting the wrong things from your airline." The first paragraph said, "Airlines have been promoting a smile, a meal and a movie so hard, for so long, that most people have come to believe that a smile, a meal and a movie are what airline service is all about."

The ad went on to mention several things more important,

including confidence in your airline. And it concluded, "There. Now that you know what an airline should do for you, all you have to do is pick an airline that can do it. At the moment we can think of only one."

How do you choose a church? What do you expect from it? Do you look for a smile, a handshake, and a friendly word? Are you satisfied to find a choir, a convenient location, and a minister with charisma? Or do you get down on your knees and ask God to lead you to truth—and then search till you find it?

There are so many churches today. How could you ever make a safe and wise choice? And why are there so many denominations? One reason is the tendency of people to follow a leader—and then when that leader dies, to go no farther in their search for truth. Another reason—a sadder reason for many of the divisions in Christianity today—is the prevailing custom of distorting Scripture, wresting it from its context, to make it support some favorite theory. I need not tell you that some religious groups today are formed only for monetary return or to avoid paying taxes.

But the sincere seeker for truth need not go wrong. He has this promise: "If any one chooses to do God's will, he will find out whether my teaching comes from God or whether I speak on my own." John 7:17, NIV.

Jesus was here speaking of His own teaching. But it applies to anyone's teaching. God will guide the man or woman who is sincere, who is willing to follow truth wherever it leads.

Too many of us are willing to follow truth only if it fits in with our plans, only if it doesn't cost anything, only if it makes no demands of us. We want truth to agree with our preconceived notions. We don't mind if truth leads us to a Saviour. But we don't want it to lead us to a Creator.

But may I just say this. Any religion that has no Creator is a dry well. If we trust the theory of evolution, of accident and chance, for our past, we shall have to trust it for our future. And that means trusting our future to chance. If we deny the account of creation, as God has recorded it for us in Genesis, we shall likely deny the future as it is predicted in the book of Revelation.

A religion without a Creator is a religion without hope. For only a Creator can change our hearts. Only a Creator can restore in us the image of God. Without a Creator there can be no resurrection. Only the One who has conquered death can call our loved ones—or us—to life. And without a Creator, the new earth described in the last two chapters of Revelation could never be a reality.

Do we want to rob Jesus of His creatorship and leave Him powerless to keep His promises? Do we want to rob the Saviour of His power to save—and leave Him just a deluded teacher who promised castles that He could never build?

I say again, a religion without a Creator is a dry well!

People change. Bad people become good. And good people become bad. Churches change too. God's chosen people became the nation that rejected Jesus. "He came unto his own, and his own received him not." John 1:11, KJV.

Those of the chosen nation who chose to *accept* Jesus had to break strong national ties and long-established customs and identify themselves with the newborn Christian church.

But, in time, the Christian church became a popularity-seeking church, a compromising church, and finally a persecuting church. The true church became the false church. It fell from its high position. It became Babylon, the symbol of all false worship. And God calls, "Come out of her, my people." Revelation 18:4, KJV.

There are times when it is not enough to believe, to know what is truth, to have right opinions, to silently place our sympathies on the right side. It was not enough for the ancient Hebrews, on that fateful night in Egypt, merely to believe. The blood had to be sprinkled on the doorpost. It was not enough for the Israelites to stand with the Red Sea before them and wait for a miracle. They must move forward!

It is not enough to say, "I believe." It is not enough to be a secret disciple of Jesus. We must step over onto the Lord's side. If we are on a sinking ship, it is not enough to *applaud* the lifeboat. We must *get into it*. It is not enough to agree that Babylon has fallen and is not what she once was. We must heed God's call and come out of her!

Today there may appear to be many options open to us. We may be confused by the multiplicity of voices all calling, "This is the way." But it will not always be so. Before Jesus returns the confusion will disappear. The issues will be plain and uncomplicated. There will be *only two camps*—those who choose to carry the banner of the fallen angel, and those who stand unflinching beneath the blood-red banner of Calvary!

Jesus said, "Other sheep I have, which are not of this fold: them also I must bring, and they shall hear my voice; and there shall be one fold, and one shepherd." John 10:16, KJV.

God's true sheep are scattered today—in many nations, many cultures, many communions—even in the fallen Babylon. And many are isolated, with no ties to any organized group. But the Saviour knows them all. And He says, "My sheep hear my voice, and I know them, and they follow me." John 10:27, KJV.

How can you tell if you are one of Jesus' true followers? You are His *if you follow Him*. That's the way to tell!

I came across a delightful little story not long ago. A boy was herding his father's sheep. Not far away, across a little valley, a neighbor boy was herding sheep for *his* father. The boys were good friends. They often called to each other across the valley that separated them.

One day a severe storm came up very suddenly, and the boys, with their sheep, took refuge under the same huge ledge. When the storm was over and it was time to go home, the boys had a problem. They couldn't separate the sheep. Some of them they knew. But they weren't sure about others.

Finally, in desperation, and fearful that they would be scolded, they started for home—one down one path and one down another. And what happened? The sheep just separated themselves perfectly, every sheep following his own shepherd!

A great dividing is going on today. The sheep, day by day, are sorting themselves out, each one following his own shepherd. And if you want to know who a sheep belongs to, who his shepherd is, just watch to see whose voice brings a response. No man has to divide them, or judge them, or classify them, or put them over here or over there. By their actions, by their responses, the sheep are separating themselves.

If you find yourself at a dry well, follow Jesus! It may mean traveling five kilometers east—or west or north or south. But you can't go wrong. You'll find living water. And a well that never goes dry!